Taxes, Financial Policy, and Small Business

Taxes, Financial Policy, and Small Business

Theodore E. Day
Vanderbilt University

Hans R. Stoll
Vanderbilt University

Robert E. Whaley
University of Alberta

Lexington Books
D.C. Heath and Company/Lexington, Massachusetts/Toronto

Library of Congress Cataloging in Publication Data
Day, Theodore E.
  Taxes, financial policy, and small business.

  Bibliography: p.
  Includes index.
  1. Small business—Taxation—United States. 2. Small business—United States—Finance.
I. Stoll, Hans R. II. Whaley, Robert E. III. Title.
HD2346.U5D39   1985   338.6′42′0973   85-40016
ISBN 0-669-10393-4 (alk. paper)

Published simultaneously in Canada
Printed in the United States of America on acid-free paper
International Standard Book Number: 0-669-10393-4
Library of Congress Catalog Card Number: 85-40016

Contents

Figures

Tables

Preface

This book presents the results of a study of small business financing and tax policy, conducted for the Small Business Administration. Federal tax policy has been the focus of much discussion and debate. This book provides empirical evidence on one aspect of the debate—namely, the differential impact of federal taxation on small and large firms. Another issue of continuing concern to policymakers is the method and the adequacy of the financing of small firms. We present empirical evidence on this issue, with particular emphasis on the impact of taxes on the choice of financing. Finally, as a measure of investor interest in small firms, we compare the returns earned by investors in small publicly held firms with the returns earned by investors in large publicly held firms.

We are grateful to the Small Business Administration for supporting the study, and in particular, we thank Charles C. Ou and Thomas A. Gray for their help. Thanks are also due to Russell E. Covey for his computer programming support and to Barbara Drake for her cheerful and diligent typing of the manuscript.

1
Toward a Theory of Small Business Finance

When questioned, small business owners frequently reply that they have no need or desire for outside equity financing. A May 1980 survey of 1,000 small firms with 40 to 500 employees, conducted for the Heller Small Business Institute by the Roper Organization, found that only 2 percent of the small businesses surveyed would sell shares as their first choice of financing. Only 20 percent would sell shares as their second choice. In contrast, 90 percent of the small businesses would borrow from a financial institution as their first financing choice. Similarly, a study by Stockwell and Byrnes (1961) found that 65 percent of the small firm respondents expressed no need for long-term debt or equity funds.

What explains this reluctance to use outside equity financing? Is it that small firms are not interested on any terms, or is it that they believe they cannot acquire equity financing on fair terms? Neither of these extreme positions is correct. Instead, rational explanations for avoiding outside equity financing are present, as is shown in this chapter. In the early to middle stages of a small firm's growth, equity financing tends to be avoided because the price received per share, while justified from the perspective of outside investors, is too low in the eyes of the small business entrepreneur and/or because the terms of the financing and the restrictions placed on managerial actions that outsiders justifiably demand are too onerous to the entrepreneur. In addition, equity financing is often avoided because the costs of acquiring it—accounting, legal, and underwriting fees—albeit justified, are too high.

When outside equity financing is acquired by firms, it is frequently the last stage in the financial growth of the firm. Initial equity capital is typically provided by the entrepreneur and by his friends and relatives. Almost immediately the entrepreneur relies upon bank loans collateralized by his personal assets and,

Note: An earlier version of this chapter appears as part of H.R. Stoll, "Small Firms' Access to Public Equity Financing," in *Studies of Small Business Finance*, Report to Congress prepared by the Interagency Task Force on Small Business Finance, Washington, D.C., February 1982.

at later stages of growth, by the firm's assets. Only when bank financing becomes excessive relative to the contributions of the entrepreneur and friends does outside public equity typically become a viable option. At that point the transaction costs of arranging a new public equity financing can become a substantial deterrent to equity financing. Our purpose is to examine the factors that give rise to this pattern of financing.

This chapter is organized as follows: The impact on the financial structure of agency costs arising from the different objectives of owners, managers, and outside suppliers of funds is examined first. Second, the role of asymmetric information is considered. Third, we examine the optimal portfolio choice of the entrepreneur and the point at which a broader equity base is required to facilitate the continued growth of the firm. Fourth, some evidence on the transaction costs of aquiring outside equity and maintaining a viable secondary market is presented. A model that incorporates the previously discussed factors affecting the financial structure and that relates these factors to the optimal size of firm is presented next. We conclude with a discussion of the implications of the analysis for financial policy of small firms.

Monitoring Costs

A large firm is a complex set of implicit contractual arrangements involving the initial owner-entrepreneur, the manager, the employees, the lenders, the suppliers, the outside equity holders, and the government. Resolving the divergent interests of these parties is costly and often reduces the flexibility of the manager. As long as the entrepreneur owns and operates the business, conflicts and the costs of resolving conflicts are avoided. As a result, entrepreneurs are reluctant to seek outside financing since it increases the number of divergent interests that must be reconciled. Similarly, outsiders are reluctant to commit funds, knowing the costs and the difficulties associated with assuring their proper use.

As Jensen and Meckling (1976) show, part of the difficulty arises from the fact that outside equity financing induces actions by the entrepreneurs that are not in the interest of the outside stockholders. Since entrepreneurs receive only a fraction of the profits when they share ownership with outside shareholders, they have an incentive to divert resources directly to themselves through consumption of perquisites or other means that reduce the return to outside owners of the firm. The costs of monitoring the owner-manager to insure that he acts in the interests of all shareholders can be substantial and are reflected in a lower share price. Since entrepreneurs know that these costs will be reflected in a lower share price, they are unwilling to sell shares unless the benefits of the greater availability of financing more than outweigh the costs.

Jensen and Meckling (1976) also show that outside debt financing changes the incentives of the entrepreneur, albeit not in the same way. In the presence of outside debt financing, the entrepreneur has an incentive to increase the risk of the firm because his equity position has limited liability. An increase in risk will not harm the entrepreneur on the downside since the maximum loss is his original investment, and it will increase expected upside gains since lenders do not share in such gains. In addition, the entrepreneur may have an incentive to dissipate collateral by paying excessive dividends or taking other similar actions.

The interests of outside suppliers of funds can be protected by careful and continuous monitoring of the actions and behavior of the owner-manager and by periodic renegotiation of the financing terms at which time penalties may be assessed for improper behavior. But monitoring and renegotiation are difficult if financing is from a large group of shareholders or creditors and if the financing is of a long-term nature. Because of the high cost of protecting the interests of outside public equity or debt holders, a cost which must be borne by the small firm, public debt or equity financing is not usually sought if other sources of financing are available.

Monitoring costs tend to be minimized when there is a single knowledgeable lender who makes short-term loans that permit periodic settling-up with the entrepreneur and who has a large enough stake in the business to warrant the necessary monitoring of the activities of the owner-manager.[1] Bank financing tends to meet these requirements. The critical role of bank loans in the financing of small businesses can be viewed as a rational attempt to avoid the adverse incentive effects of outside equity financing while at the same time minimizing the monitoring costs of debt financing.

Asymmetric Information

Each entrepreneur seeking outside funds tends to exaggerate his capabilities and the value of the project, leaving to the potential supplier of funds the task of distinguishing good credit risks from bad. This credit evaluation task requires a substantial investment in information gathering. While such an investment may be sensible for a single large supplier of funds, it is much less likely that many individual suppliers of funds participating in a public debt or equity financing would each be willing to bear such a cost. Furthermore, full disclosure by the entrepreneur of the merits of his project may compromise confidential information and bring forth competitors who bid away the superior returns of the very project being financed (see Campbell 1979).

An alternative to becoming fully informed is for the supplier of funds to demand an interest rate on loans or a price for equity shares that reflects the average quality of the firms seeking financing. Losses from bad credit risks are thereby offset by gains from good credit risks. However, each small business, having superior information about itself, is able to determine whether the rate charged or the price received accurately reflects its credit standing. If the cost of the financing is too high, the firm will either seek financing elsewhere or not seek it at all. Thus, there may be a tendency for only the poorer risks to remain in the financial market. Since the poorer risks tend to default on loans and go out of business, the supplier of funds does not earn an adequate return. The final result can be the failure of the market to provide financing to small business because suppliers of funds refuse to participate.[2]

Asymmetric information and the cost of becoming informed tend to be greatest when financing is public. Credit worthy firms therefore have an incentive to avoid public financing. As before, bank financing appears to minimize many of the difficulties. To the extent that the bank is a principal lender for the firm, it can justify the costs of becoming informed. To the extent that loans are short term, the bank can periodically reassess the validity of the claims of the entrepreneur. Moreover, continual contact between the bank and the firm can build up a sense of understanding and mutual confidence. The bank also has little incentive to use confidential information about the small firm since it cannot directly profit from such knowledge by going into business itself.

Since the bank cannot obtain perfect information about the firm, it usually also seeks to protect itself by requiring collateral. When the firm is small, the personal assets of the entrepreneur must usually be pledged. The collateral posted by the entrepreneur directly secures the loan from the bank and signals confidence in the project on the part of the entrepreneur.

The Entrepreneur's Portfolio Position

It is clear from the preceding discussion that agency costs and the costs of dealing with asymmetric information can be eliminated only if the entrepreneur finances the entire project. However, self-financing is frequently impossible because the firm must operate at a minimum scale that exceeds the resources of the entrepreneur, and even when it is possible, self-financing imposes significant costs on the entrepreneur.

First, the inability to use capital markets forces the entrepreneur to invest where the marginal internal rate of return (MIRR) on the project equals his personal marginal rate of transformation between present and future consumption. This can produce a lower level of utility than investing where MIRR equals the market rate of return and borrowing or lending to achieve the optimal consumption pattern (see Fama and Jensen 1982a).

Second, there is a cost in the form of a loss of diversification. By using a substantial fraction of his personal wealth to finance the project, the entrepreneur takes on unsystematic risk that could have been diversified away. As a result, the entrepreneur demands a higher return and operates the firm at a smaller scale than would be the case were outside financing possible.

Ragazzi (1981) shows that the loss of diversification causes the value of a closely held firm to be less than that of an identical widely held firm. He argues that there is a "rent from control" to the entrepreneur that makes him forgo the benefits of portfolio diversification. Ragazzi fails to note that if the firm were widely held, costs of dealing with agency problems and asymmetric information would be incurred that could exceed the cost attributable to the loss of diversification. These costs would reduce the value of the open corporation below that of the closed corporation. Indeed, the decision to go public hinges on the relative size of these costs.

As we have indicated, bank financing can meet some of the firm's financing needs at a lower cost than public financing. However, there are limits to bank financing. In part, these limits arise from the usual concern about adequate collateral and adequate protection against bankruptcy. In addition, they arise from the fact that a bank or other supplier of funds to a new firm views a significant investment by the entrepreneur as a signal of the entrepreneur's confidence in the project. Thus, a heavy investment by the entrepreneur (as a fraction of his wealth) and a consequent loss of diversification are likely to be necessary in the early stages of a firm's growth.

Broadening the Financial Base

The small firm will look to outside equity financing when the bank considers the financial risk to be too great and demands a broader financing base. This point may never be reached by small firms experiencing moderate growth that can be financed from retained earnings. In contrast, firms in a growth industry with substantial business risks and assets of intangible value may experience the need for a broader equity base at a much earlier stage. Thus, high technology firms with uncertain future prospects and with assets specific to the firm are more likely to need outside equity financing than service or retail establishments in well-defined markets.

A decision to seek outside equity financing imposes two rather substantial costs that many small firms are not in a position to incur. First, equity financing implies that the firm is willing to bear the costs of establishing a broader, more formal nexus of contracts specifying the rights and obligations of the inside owners, outside owners, managers, and lenders. Among other things, these costs are likely to include a more formal system of internal controls and more formal auditing and financial reporting procedures. Indeed, Fama and Jensen (1982b, 1983) emphasize that the choice of the open corporation depends on balancing higher agency costs in the open corporation against the benefits of unrestricted risk sharing and specialized management in the open corporation. Second, the use of outside equity financing implies that the firm is prepared to incur the flotation costs associated with a new issue and is confident that its stock will have a viable secondary market in which its future outside shareholders may transact at a reasonable cost. These costs are discussed in greater detail in the next section.

Venture capital financing is frequently used as an intermediate form of outside equity prior to a public issue of stock. Such financing avoids the flotation costs of a new issue and is likely to be used when a viable secondary market for the company's shares is not in the offing. Venture capital financing does carry with it increased controls on the owner-manager and formal contractual arrangements for specifying the rights and obligations of the venture capitalists, vis-à-vis the inside owners, the managers, and the lenders. Venture capital financing is more important in industries with growth potential, high risk, and assets of little collateral value. Bank lending is more limited in such industries, and a broadening of the equity base beyond the resources of the entrepreneur is likely to be necessary at an earlier stage than in industries with less risk and more collateral.

The primary benefit of outside equity financing is to provide a broad financial base for future corporate growth. A second benefit, associated with a public equity offering, accrues to the entrepreneurs who then have the opportunity to diversify their portfolios. In the start-up stage, the entrepreneur must provide personal collateral not only as security for loans but also as a signal of faith in the future of the firm. As the business expands and a more formal corporate organization is established, the need for a personal commitment of funds by the entrepreneur is reduced. The prospects of the firm and the nexus of contracts that is the firm become more important than the assets and abilities of the entrepreneur. This point is usually reached with the advent of public outside financing, and it is at this point that entrepreneurs can also choose to sell shares for their own accounts to diversify their risk out of their own firms.[3]

Transaction Costs of Public Equity Financing

The costs of outside public equity financing are of two types: (1) the flotation costs of a new issue that are paid by the issuing corporation and thus indirectly by its shareholders and (2) the secondary market transaction costs that are paid directly by shareholders.

Flotation Costs

There are two principal components to flotation costs: expenses and underwriter compensation. Expenses include legal, accounting, and engineering fees; printing costs; SEC (Securities and Exchange Commission) filing fees; state taxes and fees; and federal revenue stamps. Underwriter compensation is measured by the difference between the value of the issue sold and the proceeds received by the issuing corporation. When stated as a percentage of the proceeds, this cost is

Table 1–1
Flotation Costs, by Size of Issue, for the Years 1971 and 1972

Size of Issue ($ Million)	Number of Issues	Compensation of Underwriters as Percent of Gross Proceeds[a]	Other Expenses as Percent of Gross Proceeds[a]
Under 0.5	43	13.24	10.35
0.5–0.99	227	12.48	8.26
1–1.99	271	10.60	5.87
2–4.99	450	8.19	3.71
5–9.99	287	6.70	2.03
10–19.99	170	5.52	1.11
20–49.99	109	4.41	0.62
50–99.99	30	3.94	0.31
100–499.99	12	3.03	0.16
Over 500	0	—	—
Total/average	1,599	8.41	4.02

Source: SEC, *Cost of Flotation of Registered Issues 1971–72* (December 1974), Washington, D.C., p. 9. Reg. A issues are not included; includes seasoned and unseasoned issues.

[a]The cost ratios in each size class are calculated by an arithmetic averaging of the ratios for the firms in the class. Prior SEC studies aggregated expenses (or underwriter compensation) for all firms in a class and divided by gross proceeds of all firms in the class. The procedure used in this table tends to yield higher average ratios than the procedure used in prior SEC studies.

referred to as the *percentage spread*. Underwriter compensation covers the cost of originating and distributing the issue and, in the case of a firm commitment, the cost of bearing risk.

Numerous studies of flotation costs have been carried out by both the SEC and academic investigators. The conclusion of these studies is clear. Flotation costs, especially the expenses component, have a large fixed cost element. A large issue spreads the fixed cost over more dollars. Since small firms tend to have small issues, percentage flotation costs are greater the smaller the firm. Table 1–1 presents data on the level of flotation costs and the pattern of flotation costs according to the size of the firm. While comprehensive studies of flotation costs have not been conducted in recent periods, the evidence suggests that percentage costs would be of the same order of magnitude and exhibit the same relation to the size of the firm. Costs are clearly quite substantial for small firms—on the order of 20 percent. Moreover, for the very smallest issues, underwriters tend to reduce services, as evidenced by the fact that many offerings are on a best efforts rather than a firm commitment basis.

Since firms do not seek new equity financing annually, it is appropriate to ask what the annual cost of these periodic flotations is. Assume that a small firm is in an industry in which the annual return on real assets for large firms is 15 percent and in which large firms are able to acquire funds at a flotation cost of 5 percent. A flotation cost of 20 percent for the small firm would then imply that the annual required rate of return on investments of the small firm must be 17.8

percent, or 2.8 percent higher than on investments of the large firm. In effect, the cost of capital of the small firm is raised by 18.75 percent.[4]

Cost of Maintaining a Secondary Market

Public equity financing is possible only if investors can expect a reasonably liquid secondary market in which to trade shares. Many small firms simply never reach a size large enough to warrant the maintenance of such a secondary market. As a result, an attempt to offer new shares by such firms may be unsuccessful or may be successful only at a price that management would consider to be too low.

According to the Internal Revenue Service (IRS) statistics of income, there are approximately 13 million businesses in the United States. Of these, 11 million are proprietorships or partnerships. There are approximately 2 million corporations, of which 350,000 are Sub Chapter S corporations that are closely held and treated as partnerships for tax purposes. Of the standard corporations only about 21,000 are traded in a secondary market as follows:

Market	Number of Firms
New York Stock Exchange (NYSE)	1,500
American Stock Exchange (AMEX)	1,000
Regional Exchanges	200
NASDAQ	3,000
Non-NASDAQ OTC	15,000

Thus, it is evident that relatively few businesses are in fact able to establish a secondary market. Furthermore, the non-NASDAQ OTC market is judged to be quite inactive, with the result that only about 5,700 corporations have what would be called an active secondary market.

A measure of the cost of maintaining a secondary market for those stocks in which such a market is viable is given by the fees charged by brokers and dealers to trade shares. In a turnaround transaction, an investor would buy at the dealer's ask price and pay a commission and would subsequently sell at the dealer's bid price and pay another commission. Studies of transaction costs in the OTC market and the exchange markets make it clear that transaction costs are a function of firm size (or volume of trading, which is highly correlated with firm size). In a study of 2,214 industrial NASDAQ stocks in July 1973, Stoll (1978b) found the median spread to be 10.5 percent. Ten percent of the stocks had a spread of less than 3.79 percent, and 10 percent had a spread of greater than 25.64 percent. The investor may also have incurred commission costs and the cost of the time to investigate and analyze the company. On the NYSE, Stoll and Whaley (1983) found that the total transaction cost on a turnaround transaction in the period 1960 to 1980 averaged 6.77 percent for the smallest 10 percent of firms and 2.71 percent for the largest 10 percent of the firms. Thus, even in a market in which all firms are relatively large, the smallest firms incur substantially higher transaction costs than do the largest firms.

This difference in trading costs implies that a small corporation must earn a return (capital gain plus dividend) large enough to offset the higher transaction costs to the investor. Thus, the small firm is faced with a higher cost of capital. How much greater the return must be depends on the investor's holding period. Suppose an investor in a small company faces a turnaround transaction cost of 16 percent while an investor in a large company faces a turnaround transaction cost of 4 percent. If the holding period is one year, the small firm must earn 12 percent per year more than the large firm in order to cover the transaction cost differential, a formidable task. For an n-year holding period it must earn $12/n$ percent more. What is likely to happen is that investors in small firms will accept longer holding periods to reduce annual transaction costs but will not accept holding periods of a length sufficient to equalize annual transaction costs with those of large firms.

Suppose that the equilibrium market holding period for a small firm with a turnaround transaction cost of 16 percent is 2 years. This implies an annual transaction cost of 8 percent. Furthermore, suppose that large firms with a transaction cost of 4 percent per year have an equilibrium market holding period of 1 year. Under these assumptions and taking into account the higher flotation costs faced by small firms, what return must be earned by the small firm as compared with a large firm if both firms are operating in industries with the same underlying productivity of capital? Based on our discussion of flotation costs and secondary market trading costs, the small firm would be required to earn a return between 6 and 7 percent higher than the large firm in order to leave investors indifferent between the two types of firms. To say that the cost of capital is higher for small firms in the same industry as a large firm is not to say that the higher cost of capital is unjustified. As we have indicated, there are very real costs of establishing and maintaining a secondary market for shares.

Size of Firm and Cost of Financing

The preceding discussion of agency costs, asymmetric information, the entrepreneur's portfolio position, and the transaction costs of public equity financing suggests that the optimal pattern of financing changes as a firm grows. As we have indicated, bank financing appears to minimze many of the costs of debt financing at an early stage of the firm's growth. Assume the bank is able to determine the true return distribution of the investment project for which the entrepreneur seeks financing and that the bank, at some cost, is able to ensure that the entrepreneur does not switch to a riskier project. Thus, depending on the risk of the project and the collateral associated with the project (for example, land or machinery), the bank will lend some fraction, k, of the assets, A, required to operate

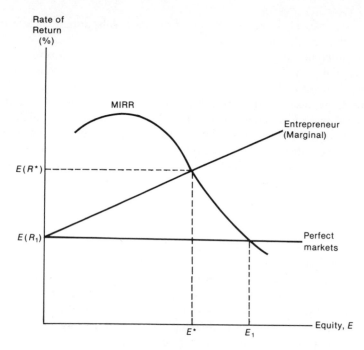

Figure 1–1. Demand for Equity and Entrepreneurial Supply of Equity

the project. The interest rate on the loan will depend on the costs of becoming informed, the agency costs of controlling the entrepreneur's behavior, and the risk of repayment of the loan.

Figure 1–1 depicts the demand for the equity funds needed to operate the project, $E = (1 - k)A$, given the existence of bank financing. The schedule labeled MIRR is the expected marginal internal rate of return to equity holders at various sizes of the firm. Beyond some point this return declines as the size of the firm increases. At early stages of growth, equity financing is provided by the entrepreneur (and friends and relatives). The marginal cost of financing by the entrepreneur is given by the upward-sloping line labeled *entrepreneur*.

The cost of equity financing from the entrepreneur consists of two components: (1) the perfect market cost of equity that outside shareholders would demand in the absence of agency costs, information costs, and transaction costs or that the entrepreneur would demand if his or her portfolio were fully diversified[5] and (2) a premium for loss of diversification that depends on the variance of returns on the equity, the entrepreneur's attitude toward risk, and the size of the entrepreneur's position in the firm relative to his wealth.[6]

The equilibrium amount of equity is E^*, and therefore, the equilibrium size of firm is $\dfrac{E^*}{1 - k}$. The cost of equity is $E(R^*)$. In perfect markets, the cost of

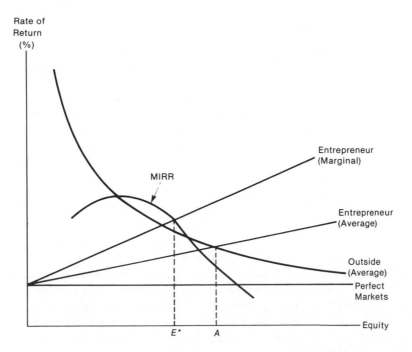

Figure 1–2. Choice between Entrepreneurial Financing and Outside Financing

equity would be $E(R_1)$; the amount of equity, E_1; and the size of firm, $\dfrac{E_1}{1 - k}$. Ragazzi (1981) argues that outsiders would pay a premium for this firm since they would discount future cash flows at $E(R_1)$ rather than $E(R^*)$. However, this is true only if there are no agency costs, information costs, or transaction costs of outside financing. However, it is precisely that because these costs are high for the small firm, the small firm must rely on financing by the entrepreneur and other informal sources.

The choice between informal inside financing and formal outside financing is depicted in figure 1–2. The average cost of outside equity financing, which is represented by the downward-sloping schedule labeled *outside*, is assumed to have two components: (1) the perfect market cost of equity financing and (2) a cost consisting primarily of fixed costs that represents agency costs, information costs, and transaction costs. At a small scale of operations, the fixed cost component is a large fraction of the outside equity supplied. At large scales of operation, the fixed cost component declines as a fraction of equity funds supplied.

The cost curve for outside financing is based on the assumption that the entrepreneur provides no equity financing (although he may participate as an employee). This assumption implies higher monitoring costs than if the entrepreneur participates in the financing. These costs imply that there is a critical size of firm below which all equity financing comes from the entrepreneur and above which all equity financing is public financing. In figure 1–2 this critical size is labeled *A*, the point at which the average costs of inside and outside financing are equal.

When a firm is started, the entrepreneur determines if the intersection of his marginal cost of equity financing and the marginal internal rate of return on the project is to the left of point *A*. If it is, financing is entirely from personal sources. This is the case depicted in figure 1–1, which we assume to be quite typical. In figure 1–2 the MIRR curve is also drawn to produce an intersection to the left of *A*. One can see in figure 1–2 that the average cost of financing E^* is higher using outside financing than it is using inside financing.

However, a MIRR schedule located farther to the right would have produced an intersection to the right of *A*. At such a point the average cost of outside financing is less than the average cost of inside financing. The entrepreneur would be better off by selling shares to the public and investing his wealth in a diversified portfolio of marketable assets. By doing so the entrepreneur avoids the personal costs associated with a loss of diversification. The entrepreneur continues to profit because of the ability to sell shares at a price that exceeds the cost of purchasing assets for the firm. The market value of his position represents the present value of the difference between the average return on the project and the average cost of funds.

When starting a business the entrepreneur may anticipate a MIRR schedule producing an intersection to the left of *A* at which inside financing is optimal. Over time the MIRR schedule may shift to the right, justifying outside financing. Such a shift produces a discontinuity in financing sources because, as soon as any outside equity financing is warranted, costs are minimized by using only outside equity. This implies that the entrepreneur will sell his stake in the firm when the switch to outside financing is justified. As pointed out earlier, insider sales frequently accompany public offerings.

Two factors have been ignored in this analysis. One is that the cost of outside financing is a function of the entrepreneur's stake in the business. Taking account of this fact implies the existence of a different schedule for the average cost of outside equity financing, one for each level of participation by the entrepreneur. This means that financing mixes that have both inside and outside financing are possible.

A second factor is that, as the entrepreneur's share of the profits declines as the participation of outsiders increases, he has an incentive to consume perquisites. We have implicitly assumed that sufficient monitoring costs are incurred by outsiders to eliminate this possibility. However, such a high level of monitoring is probably not optimal. Instead, some consumption of perquisites would probably be permitted. In our model the consumption of perquisites would be represented by a lower MIRR at each scale of operation.

Implications for the Financial Policy of Small Firms

In this chapter we have provided a theoretical framework for capital structure choice that is based on minimizing agency costs of monitoring managers, costs of dealing with asymmetric information, costs to the entrepreneur of inadequate diversification, and transaction costs of public financing. The following implications arise from the analysis:

Small firms will place greater reliance than large firms on inside equity financing by the entrepreneur and other informal sources because the fixed costs of outside equity for small firms are relatively high.

Small firms will tend to have higher debt-equity ratios than large firms, ceteris paribus, because inside equity is costly due to lost diversification.

Small firms will place greater reliance on bank financing as the source of debt because it minimizes agency and information costs of debt financing. Public debt financing imposes many of the same costs as public equity financing.

Small firms will be compelled to use a larger fraction of short-term debt relative to long-term debt than large firms because short-term debt provides a mechanism for more effective monitoring.

Notes

1. Fama (1980) emphasizes the importance of ex post settling up in disciplining managers.

2. The seminal article in this area is by Akerlof (1970). Applications to finance include Leland and Pyle (1977) and Ross (1977, 1978).

3. Approximately 30 percent of the value of initial public equity offerings are secondary sales, the proceeds of which go to initial owners or other early investors in the firm. See SEC (1980).

4. The calculation as follows:

$$(1 - c_s)k_s = (1 - c_L).15$$

$$k_s = \frac{(1 - c_L)}{(1 - c_s)} .15 = \frac{1 - .05}{1 - .20} .15 = (1.1875)(.15) = .178$$

where c_s, c_L are proportional flotation cost of large and small firms, respectively, and k_s = cost of capital of small firms.

5. Under the Sharpe-Lintner capital asset pricing model, this cost is given by

$$E(R_i) = R_f + [E(R_m) - R_f]\beta_i ,$$

where

$$R_f = \text{risk-free rate,}$$
$$E(R_m) = \text{return on the market,}$$
$$\beta_i = \beta \text{ coefficient of the equity of the firm.}$$

6. The underlying theory is contained in Stoll (1978). The problem of the dealer who takes on a large inventory position in return for a higher expected return is the same as that of the entrepreneur who takes on a large position in his firm in return for a higher expected return on the investment.

2
Taxes and Financial Policy

Chapter 1 analyzed some of the factors influencing financial policy in the absence of taxes. We argued that agency costs, costs of dealing with asymmetric information, and transaction costs of public financing cause small firms to rely on informal equity financing by the entrepreneur and close associates and debt financing in the form of short-term bank loans. Moreover, because sufficient informal equity financing may not be available, we hypothesized that small firms rely more heavily on debt financing (from a bank) than large firms in the same industry.

Taxes have an important additional effect on firms' financial policies. The purpose of this chapter is to analyze the effect of federal taxation on financial policy. We begin with a review of the literature on taxes and financial policy. This review is followed by the discussion of a theoretical framework that emphasizes the interaction of taxes and firm size in the determination of the firm's leverage and dividend policy.

Review of the Literature

Taxes and the Debt-Equity Ratio

Modigliani and Miller (1958) rigorously analyze the effect of corporate debt on the value of the firm. They show that, in the absence of taxes and other market imperfections, the total value of a firm is unaffected by the amount of debt in its capital structure. In a later paper Modigliani and Miller (1963) show that, when corporate taxes are considered, corporate borrowing increases the value of the firm. Interest expense can be deducted from net operating income when the firm's tax liability is computed so the leverage premium is equal to the present value of the future tax shields of the firm's long-term debt or, more simply, the corporate tax rate times the market value of the firm's bonds. Modigliani and Miller (1963) are careful to note that their analysis does not imply that firms should use the maximum level of debt possible. They suggest that the firm's optimal capital structure might also be affected by additional considerations such as the need to preserve flexibility, personal taxes, uncertainty associated with the tax savings from debt, and creditor's concern about bankruptcy.

Brennan and Schwartz (1978) examine the loss of the tax benefits of debt that occurs when a firm becomes insolvent. Additional debt in the firm's capital structure has two offsetting effects on the value of the firm: (1) an increase in the potential interest tax savings and (2) an increase in the probability of subsequent insolvency. The interaction of these two effects suggests that the value-maximizing capital structure will include both debt and equity. All else constant, Brennan and Schwartz show, by means of a simulation, that the optimal level of debt for a firm decreases as the cost of bankruptcy and the business risk of the firm increase. It is worthwhile to note that Kraus and Litzenberger (1973) reach similar conclusions by examining the market price of tax shields and bankruptcy costs in a state-preference framework.

In contrast, Miller (1977) argues that the importance of bankruptcy costs in determining a firm's optimal capital structure is overstated. To support his assertion, he cites a study by Warner (1977) that shows that the costs of bankruptcy for a sample of railroads that filed bankruptcy petitions from 1930 through 1955 averaged only 5.3 percent of the market value of the firm's securities as of the filing date. Miller goes on to analyze the role of personal taxes in determining the firm's optimal capital structure. The paper emphasizes the trade-off between the corporate tax advantage of issuing debt and the personal tax disadvantage of receiving interest income, which is taxed at a higher rate than the combination of dividend and capital gains income received by stockholders. Miller argues that the personal tax disadvantage in receiving the interest income from corporate debt causes the level of debt in a firm's capital structure to be a matter of indifference to the shareholders of the firm. This conclusion is based on the assumption that firms will supply debt to the marketplace until the corporate tax advantage to debt is exactly offset by the personal tax disadvantage associated with the receipt of interest income.

DeAngelo and Masulis (1980) extend Miller's work by explicitly considering the role of nondebt tax shields such as depreciation and the investment tax credit in the firm's capital structure decision. Since depreciation expense and investment tax credits are tax shield substitutes for interest expense, an increase in the amount of debt in the firm's capital structure increases the probability that the firm may be unable to use all of its tax shields in a given year, which, in turn, reduces the expected value of the firm's nondebt tax shields. Consequently, a change in the firm's capital structure will, in general, affect the value of the firm.

The DeAngelo and Masulis model predicts that, as corporate taxes are increased, firms will substitute debt for equity, due to the increased value per dollar of tax shields. Furthermore, at any point in time, firms subject to lower corporate tax rates will normally have less debt in their capital structures. The analysis is supported by the fact that differences in capital structure across industries seem to be explained by the ratio of nondebt tax shields to earnings before interest and taxes and by the observation that firms within an industry tend, on average, to have similar capital structures.

Cordes and Sheffrin (1983) have estimated the change in corporate tax liability caused by an increase in interest expense using the Treasury Corporate Tax Model. Their results indicate that incremental interest deductions impair the ability of some firms to make full use of nondebt tax shields. The two most important sources of this loss arise from the inability of firms to make full use of the foreign tax credit and the investment tax credit when debt is added to the capital structure. Cordes and Sheffrin find that, on average, the effective tax advantage of an additional dollar of interest deductions is 31¢ rather than the statutory tax advantage of 46¢. A breakdown of the data by firm size shows that firms with assets greater than $25 million realize average tax benefits of 30 to 37¢ per additional dollar of interest deduction. In contrast, small firms (those with assets less than $1 million) normally realize only 15¢ of tax benefits for each additional dollar of interest deductions. As might be expected, the marginal benefit of additional interest deductions was found to increase with the firm's taxable income. A breakdown of the results by industry reveals a marked difference among the ability of firms within different industries to make use of additional interest deductions. The marginal benefits of debt range from 17¢ in agriculture and mining and extraction to 46¢ in tobacco manufacturing.

Both the Miller and the DeAngelo and Masulis studies analyze the firm's capital structure decision in a single period framework, which requires the assumption that all income derived from the firm's shares (that is, dividends and capital gains) is taxed at a single rate. Litzenberger and Van Horne (1978) develop a multiperiod framework that takes account of the fact that both dividend and interest income are taxed as ordinary income. The model incorporates a constraint on the sources and uses of funds to imply that a change in the firm's capital structure may alter the firm's dividend policy. This effect occurs because a change in interest expense represents a change in a use of funds that must be offset by either a change in dividends or a change in external financing. Litzenberger and Van Horne also examine the effects that two specific proposals to eliminate the double taxation of dividends might have on a firm's capital structure.

Taxes and Dividend Policy

Miller and Modigliani (1961) show that in a world without taxes, a corporation's dividend policy does not affect the value of the firm. Conversely, in a world in which capital gains are taxed at a lower rate than dividends, investors would minimize their tax liability by holding shares in firms with low dividend payouts.

Thus, firms with high dividend payouts require higher before-tax returns to give investors the same after-tax return they would earn by investing in similar firms with low dividend payouts.

This prediction is one of the results of Brennan's (1971a, 1970b) capital asset pricing model. His model explicitly considers the differential personal taxation of dividends and capital gains in a world where investors are subject to different tax rates. Brennan shows that the equilibrium expected return on a security is

$$E(\tilde{R}_i) - r_f = \beta_i [E(\tilde{R}_m) - r_f - T(d_m - r_f)] + T(d_i - r_f),$$

where

$$
\begin{aligned}
\beta_i &= \text{the } \beta \text{ coefficient of security } i, \\
E(\tilde{R}_i) &= \text{the expected return on security } i, \\
E(\tilde{R}_m) &= \text{the expected return on the market portfolio,} \\
d_m &= \text{the dividend yield on the market portfolio,} \\
d_i &= \text{the dividend yield on security } i, \\
r_f &= \text{the risk-free rate of interest,}
\end{aligned}
$$

and

$$T = \frac{T_d - T_g}{1 - T_g}$$

where

$$
\begin{aligned}
T_d &= \text{a weighted average of an individual's tax rates on} \\
&\quad \text{dividend income,} \\
T_g &= \text{a weighted average of an individual's tax rates on} \\
&\quad \text{capital gains.}
\end{aligned}
$$

If all investors pay a higher tax on dividend income than on capital gains, the model predicts that before-tax returns are positively related to dividend yield since T, as it is defined, will be unambiguously positive. However, as noted by Litzenberger and Ramaswamy (1979) and Gordon and Bradford (1980), among others, some investors, such as corporations and nonprofit organizations, are subject to little or no tax on dividend income. Thus, the effect of dividend policy on the value of the firm, at least as it is specified within the Brennan model, is an open question.

Black and Scholes (1974) argue that, in market equilibrium, firms will supply dividends in the exact amount desired by investors; that is, the supply of shares at each level of dividend yield will be equal to the demand for shares at that level of dividend yield. Consequently, no firm will have an incentive to change its dividend policy. Black and Scholes test this hypothesis by examining the relation of return and dividend yield for 25 portfolios that were constructed to have a wide range of dividend yields. Their results indicate that dividend yield is not a significant factor in explaining security returns.

Miller and Scholes (1978) assert that investors are able to offset dividend income with the deduction for interest expense generated by personal leverage. In this scenario, investors with taxable dividend income generate offsetting deductions for interest expense by borrowing. These borrowed funds can be invested at the risk-free rate of interest in tax-exempt funds [such as IRA (Individual Retirement Account) or Keough funds] or in a tax-sheltered annuity so that investors can offset dividend income with interest expense without affecting the risk of their investment portfolio. Consequently, dividend yield should not affect security returns.

Litzenberger and Ramaswamy (1979) derive and test an after-tax capital asset pricing model that accounts for the progressive nature of the personal income tax. Their empirical tests differ from those of Black and Scholes (1974) in two respects. First, rather than grouping securities into portfolios, Litzenberger and Ramaswamy estimate the relationship between before-tax return and dividend yield for individual securities. Second, Litzenberger and Ramaswamy test the significance of a dividend yield variable that is zero in any month in which the stock does not go exdividend. This is in contrast to the use of the average monthly dividend over the preceding 12 months that Black and Scholes used to proxy for a security's expected dividend yield. In contrast to Black and Scholes, the Litzenberger-Ramaswamy results suggest that there is a significant and positive relation between before-tax expected return and the dividend yield of common stocks (that is, investors on balance have a preference for capital gains).

Gordon and Bradford (1980) use a method similar to that of Litzenberger and Ramaswamy to examine the time series behavior of the market price of dividends relative to capital gains. The methodology differs from that of Litzenberger and Ramaswamy in that a weighted average of past dividends is used as an instrumental variable for expected dividends. They conclude that the capital gain that the market regards as a substitute for a dollar of dividends follows a cyclical pattern about one. The procyclical variation of this ratio with the business cycle is consistent with an interpretation of the relative price of capital gains as a marginal Tobin's q ratio. Although a relative price of one is inconsistent with a preference by investors for capital gains (due to the favorable tax treatment), Gordon and Bradford conclude that a value of one is consistent with maximizing behavior of the firm since firms intent on maximizing value would choose to supply investors with the form of return that they value most highly. This interpretation is also consistent with the supply effect described by Black and Scholes.

The evidence on the existence of yield-related tax effects by Litzenberger and Ramaswamy, Gordon and Bradford, and others is questioned by Miller and Scholes (1982). They contend that the empirical significance of dividend yield in the empirical studies is suspect because the tests do not identify instances in which a firm fails to declare an expected dividend. Such occurrences usually represent negative information about the firm and result in a decline in the price of the firm's shares. Miller and Scholes present evidence to show that the failure to identify these events causes the lower return (relative to firms that have declared a dividend) of these firms to be attributed to a tax effect. They show that a long-run definition of expected dividend yield, like the average of the previous year's dividends used by Black and Scholes eliminates the tax effects of dividend yield.

The differential taxation of dividend income and capital gains provides an incentive for investors in different marginal tax brackets to invest in firms with particular dividend policies. For instance, investors in low marginal tax brackets (for example, tax-exempt institutions) might prefer to invest in high dividend yield firms while investors in high marginal tax brackets would prefer to invest in firms with a low dividend yield.

Feldstein and Green (1983) argue that investors in a particular tax bracket will not concentrate their holdings in firms with a particular dividend payout policy. They show that when security returns are uncertain, investors choose to diversify their portfolios at the cost of earning dividend income taxable at ordinary rates. In this framework, firms maximize share price by attracting investors from different marginal tax brackets. Thus, the Feldstein and Green model explains both the fact that most companies pay a dividend and the fact that investors do not typically specialize their portfolios in firms with particular dividend payouts.

Thus far, this chapter has described the development of the literature pertaining to the role of taxes in the firm's leverage and dividend decisions. In addition, it has summarized several controversies in this area. The remainder of the chapter is devoted to developing a theoretical framework for many of the issues that have been raised and for an issue that has not been raised—namely, the role of firm size in the selection of value-maximizing dividend and leverage policies.

Theoretical Framework

The effects of leverage and dividend policy, corporate taxation, and personal taxation (more specifically, the taxation of dividends and capital gains) on the value of the firm are examined in this section. The analytical framework developed considers the relationship between the effective tax rate on business income and firm size, as well as the differences in personal tax rates across investors. The approach is based on the work reviewed in the first part of the chapter, particularly the studies by Miller (1977), Litzenberger and Van Horne (1978), Miller and Scholes (1978), DeAngelo and Masulis (1980), and Black and Scholes (1974). Firms are characterized by their corporate tax rates, by the availability of corporate tax deductions and credits, and by financial policy. Financial policy is defined by the firm's leverage and dividend payout. Individuals are characterized by their marginal personal tax rates and by their marginal capital gains rates.

The model has a single period framework. At the beginning of the period, the firm issues debt and equity. The proceeds, A, are invested in productive assets that generate before-tax operating cash flows of $\tilde{C}$. At the end of the period, bondholders receive interest payments of I dollars, and stockholders receive dividends of D dollars. Since dividends are determined prior to the realization of $\tilde{C}$, the firm's dividend payout will not be equal to the firm's after-tax net income. The residual (either positive or negative) is assumed to be converted into capital gains (or losses) that are distributed to shareholders by repurchasing shares or other procedures.

Shareholder income in the form of capital gains is defined by the cash flow identity,

$$\tilde{G} = (1 - t_c)(\tilde{C} - I - N) - D \qquad \text{for } \tilde{C} > I + N, \qquad (2.1)$$
$$\tilde{G} = \tilde{C} - I - N - D \qquad \text{for } \tilde{C} \leq I + N,$$

where

$\tilde{C}$ = before-tax cash flow from operations;
I = total interest payments to bondholders, assumed certain;
D = total dividend payments to shareholders, assumed certain;
t_c = the corporate tax rate;
N = deductible expenditures for the replacement of assets used up in production.

Full use of the tax deduction for interest expense is possible only if stockholder earnings are positive, which occurs if the before-tax operating cash flow (C) exceeds interest obligations plus depreciation expense $(I + N)$.[1] This situation is illustrated in figure 2–1 in which a probability distribution of before-tax operating cash flows is plotted. Full tax deduction of interest expense is possible only if the realization of C is to the right of point $I + N$. If $C < N$, the entire interest deduction is lost (assuming no loss carryforward).[2] There is an intermediate case—$N < C < I + N$—in which earnings partially cover interest charges so that only part of the tax deduction for interest expense is lost. We will assume that $C > 0$.

The implication of this analysis is that, unless a firm is certain to have positive earnings after interest and depreciation, the after-tax interest expense exceeds $(1 - t_c)I$. To reflect this phenomenon, we define an effective tax rate, τ_c, as follows:

$$\tau_c = \Pi t_c,$$

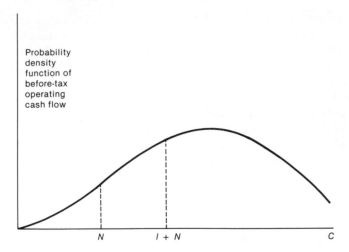

Figure 2–1. Probability Density of Before-Tax Operating Cash Flow, C

where Π is the probability that the condition $C > I + N$ is realized. In general, the effective corporate tax rate will be a function of the firm's tax deductions for interest expense [that is, $\tau_c = \tau_c(I)$]. The empirical analysis that follows examines the cross-sectional relationship between effective corporate tax rates and firm size.

Given this framework, the value of the firm is the discounted value of the initial capital of the firm (A) and the value of the expected income to be received by the holders of debt and equity at the end of the period,

$$V = A + \phi_1 I + \phi_2 D + \phi_3 \bar{G}, \qquad (2.2)$$

where

$\bar{G}$ = the expected value of residual net income (after dividend payout),
ϕ_1 = the price per dollar of interest income,
ϕ_2 = the price per dollar of dividend income,
ϕ_3 = the price per dollar of expected capital gains and losses.

The expected value of capital gains, $\bar{G}$, may be expressed [using equation (2.1)] as

$$\bar{G} = (\bar{C} - T - N) - (1 - \tau_c)I - D, \qquad (2.3)$$

where $\bar{C}$ denotes the firm's expected before-tax cash flow and T represents the expected tax liability of a firm with no debt in its capital structure. The term (1

$- \tau_c)I$ reflects the expected after-tax cost of the debt in the firm's capital structure.

Substituting equation (2.3) into equation (2.2) gives

$$V = A + I[\phi_1 - (1 - \tau_c)\phi_3] + D(\phi_2 - \phi_3) + \phi_3(\bar{C} - T - N). \quad (2.4)$$

Equation (2.4) expresses the value of the firm as a function of the firm's leverage and dividend policy and the expected after-tax cash flow of an unleveraged firm. Holding dividends constant, the effect of a small change in interest expense on the firm's value is (see the appendix)

$$\frac{\partial V}{\partial I} = \phi_1 - [1 - \tau_c(I)]\phi_3. \quad (2.5)$$

Holding leverage (and, thus, I) constant, the effect of a small change in dividends is

$$\frac{\partial V}{\partial D} = (\phi_2 - \phi_3). \quad (2.6)$$

Equations (2.5) and (2.6) emphasize the fact that the effects of leverage and dividend policy depend on prices in the capital markets and on the corporation's tax rate. Since the tax rate on capital gains is less than the tax rate on dividend income, the price of capital gains (ϕ_3) should be greater than the price of dividends (ϕ_2). Consequently, given our initial assumptions, the value of the firm should decrease as the firm increases dividends $\left(\frac{\partial V}{\partial D} < 0\right)$. This result is consistent with the work of Miller and Modigliani (1961) and others. We analyze empirically how this result is affected when we have accounted for the explicit differences in firm size. The relationship of firm value to leverage (that is, the sign of $\frac{\partial V}{\partial I}$) requires further description of the supply and demand of securities in the capital markets.

In complete and perfect markets, the expected after-tax yield to an investor on claims to the firm's cash flows are as follows:

$$\text{Debt: } \frac{(1 - \tau)}{\phi_1},$$

$$\text{Dividends: } \frac{(1 - \tau)}{\phi_2},$$

$$\text{Capital gains: } \frac{(1 - \tau_g)}{\phi_3},$$

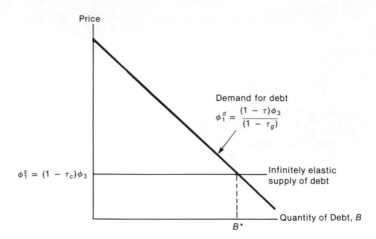

Figure 2–2. Supply and Demand for Debt: Homogeneous Corporate Tax Rates

where

τ = the tax rate on ordinary income,
τ_g = the tax rate on capital gains.

Under current tax law, interest and dividend income are taxed at the same rate, so that

$$\phi_1 = \phi_2.$$

Given the price of capital gains, the investor's demand price for interest income, ϕ_1^d (or dividend income, since $\phi_1 = \phi_2$), must satisfy

$$\frac{1 - \tau}{\phi_1^d} = \frac{1 - \tau_g}{\phi_3}; \tag{2.7}$$

that is, the after-tax return from interest income and capital gains income must be equalized. The demand price is then

$$\phi_1^d = \frac{(1 - \tau)\phi_3}{1 - \tau_g} \tag{2.8}$$

and is depicted in figure 2–2. Investors in low ordinary income tax brackets enjoy a higher after-tax yield on debt than investors in high ordinary income tax brackets. Thus, at high values of ϕ_1^d, only low tax investors hold debt. As the price of debt falls (yield increases), investors in higher tax brackets are willing to hold debt, and the demand for debt increases as shown in figure 2–2.

The equilibrium capital structure of a value-maximizing firm must satisfy the equation

$$\frac{\partial V}{\partial I} = 0,$$

which implies from equation (2.5) that the supply price of debt, ϕ_1^s, is

$$\phi_1^s = [1 - \tau_c(I)]\phi_3. \tag{2.9}$$

If the effective corporate tax rate, τ_c, is independent of the level of debt and is the same for all firms, then the supply of debt will be infinitely elastic as shown in figure 2–2. Thus, firms will supply any quantity of debt demanded by investors at the after-tax opportunity cost of debt. This is the case described by Miller (1977). More generally, the effective corporate tax rate of a firm is a function of its level of debt as indicated in equation (2.9). The effective tax rate for any corporation depends not only on the statutory tax rate but also on the probability of having sufficient income against which to deduct all interest payments. This probability declines with increases in debt, and as a result, τ_c is a decreasing function of a firm's level of debt. Each firm thus has an upward-sloping supply schedule of debt (which may be entirely above the equilibrium price of debt if the statutory tax rate, t_c, is sufficiently small) that yields an optimal capital structure for the individual firm. As a result, the aggregate supply of debt is also upward sloping and is shown in figure 2–3. This case has been discussed by DeAngelo and Masulis (1980).

The market equilibrium quantity of debt, B^*, and the equilibrium price, ϕ_1°, are determined such that $\phi_1^d = \phi_1^s$. When all corporations face a given corporate tax rate, there is a unique equilibrium aggregate quantity of debt, B^*, as depicted in figure 2–2, but there is not an optimal debt level for the individual firm. At the equilibrium

$$1 - \tau_c = \frac{1 - \tau^\mu}{1 - \tau_g^\mu}, \tag{2.10}$$

where τ_c is a given corporate tax rate and μ denotes the marginal investor.

When the corporate tax rate of firms depends on their level of debt, which is the case we analyze in this book, equilibrium is as depicted in figure 2–3. The market equilibrium price and quantity of debt are determined such that

$$1 - \tau^\mu = (1 - \tau_c^*)(1 - \tau_g^\mu),$$

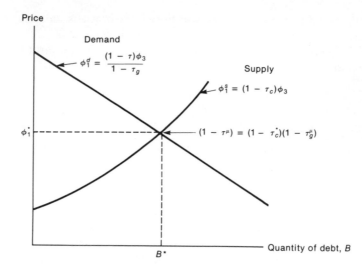

Price

Demand

$$\phi_1^d = \frac{(1 - \tau)\phi_3}{1 - \tau_g}$$

Supply

$$\phi_1^s = (1 - \tau_c)\phi_3$$

$$\phi_1^* \qquad (1 - \tau^\mu) = (1 - \tau_c^*)(1 - \tau_g^\mu)$$

B^*

Quantity of debt, B

Figure 2–3. Supply and Demand for Debt: Heterogeneous Corporate Tax Rates

where τ_c^* is the marginal effective tax rate at the optimal level of debt that causes equation (2.9) to be satisfied. Firms with low effective tax rates, resulting from low statutory tax rates and/or low probabilities of having income against which to deduct interest expense, would tend to have less debt than firms with high effective tax rates. One objective of this study is to determine effective tax rates of small businesses as compared with large businesses and to assess the impact of differences in effective tax rates for differences in capital structures.

Conclusion

This chapter has considered the role of firm size and taxation in the firm's choice of optimal (value-maximizing) leverage and dividend policies. The first section traced the development of an extensive literature on the effect of taxation in the formulation of leverage and dividend policy. This section also highlighted the current controversies in this area of research. The second section examined the role of firm size in a theoretical model that incorporates the most important features of the literature on taxation, leverage, and dividends. The model considers the fact that the tax shields from corporate debt are less valuable to small firms than large firms since they have a lower effective marginal tax rate.

The effects of taxes on the dividend and leverage decisions of a firm of a given size have been shown to depend upon the relative prices of interest income and capital gains in the marketplace. This is essentially a macroeconomic approach in the sense that the firm's financial policy is determined by economywide aggregates (namely, market prices).

Chapter 3 considers the firm's leverage decision from a somewhat different perspective. The theoretical model developed explicitly considers the role of size-related differences in income variability in the determination of a firm's optimal capital structure. In addition, the effect of differences in the cost of debt to large and small firms is considered.

Notes

1. Although the current tax code allows losses to be carried forward, the future tax benefits are not adjusted to reflect the interest cost arising from the delay in the use of deductions.

2. The assumption of symmetric tax treatment of capital gains and losses is not totally accurate, but it is satisfactory for our purposes. For the most part, our analysis assumes that firms can generate positive capital gains.

Appendix 2A
Optimal Capital Structure

The value of the firm is expressed in equation (2.2) as

$$V = A + \phi_1 I + \phi_2 D + \phi_3 \bar{G} \qquad \text{(A2.1)}$$

with

$$\bar{G} = \int_0^{I + N} (C - I - N - D)f(C)dC$$
$$+ \int_{I + N}^{\infty} [(1 - t_c)(C - I - N) - D]f(C)dC, \qquad \text{(A2.2)}$$

where the density function for C in (A2.2) is denoted by $f(C)$.

Holding dividends constant, the effect of a small change in interest expense on the value of the firm is

$$\frac{\partial V}{\partial I} = \phi_1 + \phi_3 \frac{\partial \bar{G}}{\partial I}. \qquad \text{(A2.3)}$$

Differentiating equation (A2.2) with respect to I gives

$$\frac{\partial \bar{G}}{\partial I} = [-Df(I + N) + Df(I + N)]$$
$$- \int_0^{I + N} f(C)dC - (1 - t_c) \int_{I + N}^{\infty} f(C)dC \qquad \text{(A2.4)}$$
$$= -[1 - \tau_c(I)],$$

where

$$\tau_c(I) = t_c \Pi = t_c \int_{I + N}^{\infty} f(C)dC.$$

Substituting (A2.4) into (A2.3) gives

$$\frac{\partial V}{\partial I} = \phi_1 - [1 - \tau_c(I)]\phi_3 , \tag{A2.5}$$

which is equation (2.5).

The firm's optimal capital structure is determined by the level of interest expense (I^*) that gives

$$\phi_1^s = [1 - \tau_c(I^*)]\phi_3. \tag{A2.6}$$

Differentiating ϕ_1^s with respect to I^* gives

$$\frac{\partial \phi_1^s}{\partial I^*} = t_c\phi_3 f(N + I^*) > 0, \tag{A2.7}$$

which verifies that the firm's supply curve for debt is upward sloping.

3
A Microeconomic Model of Firm Size and Capital Structure

T he analytical framework examined in chapter 2 predicts that a firm's leverage and dividend policies are related to the market prices of interest income and capital gains and to the corporation's tax rate. Thus, firm size should be a determining factor in a firm's leverage and dividend decisions due to the fact that large firms tend to have a higher corporate tax rate than small firms. This chapter analyzes the firm's leverage decision from a somewhat different perspective. The model developed takes the firm's dividend decision as given, focusing instead on the role of firm size and the variability of operating revenues in the determination of an optimal capital structure.

As DeAngelo and Masulis (1980) note, the tax deduction for interest expense is a substitute for the deduction for depreciation expense. An increase in the amount of debt in a firm's capital structure increases the probability that a firm will be unable to make full use of both deductions because operating income is uncertain. Consequently, DeAngelo and Masulis suggest that the variability of the firm's earnings stream places a limit on the amount of debt in its capital structure.

This chapter examines how this limit is related to the size of the firm. In particular, it examines the role of firm size and income variability in determining the proportion of debt in a firm's capital structure. These issues are analyzed using a model in which large firms are characterized as being portfolios of subsidiaries. Each of the subsidiaries is assumed to have size and income variability characteristics similar to those of small firms. The operating income of these subsidiaries is assumed to be less than perfectly positively correlated, which implies that large firms can achieve a so-called diversification effect that is not available to small firms. This diversification is shown to affect the ability of a firm to make full use of the tax shields from debt.

Income, Income Variability, and Firm Size

Assume that a small firm generates net operating income before depreciation (henceforth referred to as cash flow) using a production function of the form

$$\tilde{C} = \tilde{\theta}K,$$

where

$\tilde{C}$ = cash flow (net operating income before depreciation),
$\tilde{\theta}$ = the productivity of capital,
K = the quantity of capital employed by the small firm,

and $\tilde{}$ is used to indicate that C and θ are uncertain. The expected cash flow of the small firm is denoted by

$$\bar{C} = \bar{\theta}K$$

and the variance by

$$\text{Var}(\tilde{C}) = K^2\sigma^2,$$

where

σ^2 = the variance of the productivity of capital.

Large firms frequently consist of a number of subsidiaries or divisions under the control of a parent company. The operations of these component parts are summarized by the consolidated financial statements of a single reporting entity. In a sense, then, a large firm can be thought of in terms of an aggregation or a portfolio of divisions or subsidiaries. To be more precise, assume that a large firm with N divisions is a portfolio of small firms having a mean cash flow of

$$\bar{C}_N = \sum_{i=1}^{N} \bar{\theta}_i K_i \, ,$$

where

$\bar{\theta}_i$ = the mean productivity of capital for division i of the large firm,
K_i = the capital of division i of the large firm,
N = the number of small firms or divisions in the large firm.

Small firms and subsidiaries are assumed to be standardized in the sense that

$$\bar{\theta}_i = \bar{\theta} \qquad \text{for all } i,$$

and

$$K_i = K \qquad \text{for all } i.$$

In addition, the productivity of capital of the small firms or divisions is assumed to have a multivariate normal distribution with

$$\sigma_i^2 = \sigma^2 \qquad \text{for all } i$$

and

$$\text{COV}(\tilde{\theta}_i, \tilde{\theta}_j) = \sigma_{ij} = \rho\sigma^2 \qquad \text{for all } i \neq j,$$

where

ρ = the correlation coefficient between the productivity of any two firm components, i and j, with $0 < \rho < 1$.

The standardization of small firms or component divisions in terms of their size and productivity of capital provides a tractable device for the comparison of the income variability of large and small firms. This assumption can be relaxed to allow the capital intensity and mean productivity of the subsidiaries of the large firm to differ from those of small firms. Given these assumptions, the cash flow of a large firm of size N will have a normal distribution with mean

$$\bar{C}_N = N\bar{\theta}K$$

and variance[1]

$$\sigma_N^2 = N^2 K^2 \sigma^2 \left[\rho + \frac{1}{N}(1 - \rho) \right].$$

Firms have two types of tax deductions: interest expense and depreciation expense. The productive capacity of a small firm is assumed to depreciate at a rate of α per period. Consequently, a small firm has a deduction for depreciation expense of αK while a firm of size N has depreciation expense of $N\alpha K$.

A firm's interest expense accrues at a coupon rate of r on the book value of its debt, D. The total tax deductions of large and small firms are respectively[2]

$$F_N = N\alpha K + NrD_N$$

and

$$F_S = \alpha K + rD_S ,$$

where

D_S = the debt of a small firm,

D_N = the quantity of debt used to finance each division of a firm composed of N divisions (that is, total debt = ND_N).

A small firm fails to fully use the tax deduction for interest expense whenever its cash flow falls below F_s—that is, whenever

$$\tilde{C} < \alpha K + rD_S.$$

Similarly, a firm of size N is unable to take the full deduction for interest expense whenever

$$\sum_{i=1}^{N} \tilde{C}_i < N\alpha K + NrD_N.$$

Optimal Debt Level

To derive a firm's book value debt to total assets ratio as a function of firm size and income variability, firms are assumed to choose a level of debt that assures that all tax deductions will be fully used with a given level of confidence (that is, a given probability). Given the assumption that the productivity of capital for small firms has a multivariate normal distribution, this implies that the firm's capital structure decision is analogous to choosing a debt level such that expected cash flow exceeds total tax deductions by a given number of standard deviations.

Formally, this implies that the amount of debt in a small firm's capital structure will satisfy

$$\bar{\theta}K - \alpha K - rD_S = t\sigma K, \qquad (3.1)$$

where t is the number of standard deviations by which expected cash flow must exceed total deductions in order to assure that all tax deductions will be used with a given probability. For a firm of size N, this criterion implies that

$$N\bar{\theta}K - N\alpha K - NrD_N = tN\sigma K \left[\rho + \frac{1}{N}(1 - \rho) \right]^{1/2}. \qquad (3.2)$$

Equations (3.1) and (3.2) can be rearranged to give

$$\frac{D_S}{K} = \frac{1}{r}[(\bar{\theta} - \alpha) - t\sigma] \qquad (3.3)$$

and

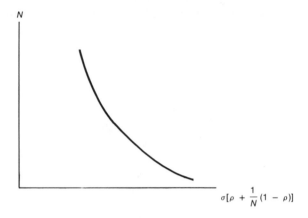

Figure 3–1. Relation of Firm Size and Standard Deviation of Funds Flow

$$\frac{D_N}{K} = \frac{1}{r} \left\{ (\bar{\theta} - \alpha) - t\sigma \left[\rho + \frac{1}{N}(1 - \rho) \right]^{1/2} \right\}. \qquad (3.4)$$

Equations (3.3) and (3.4) express the book value debt to total assets ratio as a function of firm size and the variability of income, as well as the coupon rate on debt, mean productivity, and the rate at which capital depreciates.[3] Note that when $N = 1$, equation (3.4) is identical to (3.3).

Firm size has been characterized by N, the number of divisions or subsidiaries that comprises the parent company. Differentiating (3.4) with respect to N gives

$$\frac{\partial(D/K)}{\partial N} = \frac{(1 - \rho)}{N^2} \frac{t\sigma}{2r} \left[\rho + \frac{1}{N}(1 - \rho) \right]^{-1/2} > 0. \qquad (3.5)$$

Equation (3.5) implies that as the size of the firm increases, the capacity of the firm to use the tax shields from corporate debt fully increases; that is, all else being equal, large firms tend to borrow more, as a proportion of total assets, than small firms. This tendency is the result of a diversification effect, similar to the elimination of unsystematic risk in a diversified portfolio of common stocks. This effect is illustrated by figure 3–1.

When the cash flows to the subsidiaries of a large firm are less than perfectly correlated, then on average, the cash flow of the parent company will be stabler, relative to the tax shields from depreciation and interest expense, than the cash flow of a small firm. As in portfolio diversification, there is a concave relationship between variability relative to total assets and firm size. Thus, the rate at which the relative variability is reduced as subsidiaries are added to the firm is a decreasing function of firm size. This is confirmed by the fact that

$$\frac{\partial^2 (D/K)}{\partial N^2} < 0 \qquad \text{for all } \rho > 0.$$

The importance of the diversification effect depends on the correlation of the cash flows of the large firm's subsidiaries. Equations (3.3) and (3.4) show that when cash flows are perfectly correlated across subsidiaries (that is, $\rho = 1$), a firm of any size N will choose the same debt to total assets ratio as a small firm. Differentiating (3.4) with respect to ρ gives the relation between the correlation of cash flow across subsidiaries and capital structure,

$$\frac{\partial (D/K)}{\partial \rho} = \frac{-1}{2} \frac{t\sigma}{r} \left(\frac{N-1}{N} \right) \left[\rho + \frac{1}{N}(1 - \rho) \right]^{1/2} < 0. \qquad (3.6)$$

Equation (3.6) shows that a firm's debt to total assets ratio will decrease as the correlation of cash flows across subsidiaries increases; that is, as ρ increases, the cash flow of a firm of any size N becomes less stable, which implies that the firm must choose a lower debt to total assets ratio to maintain a given probability that all tax shields will be fully used.

The effect of firm size (N) and the correlation of subsidary cash flows on the firm's optimal debt to total assets ratio is measured by the term $\sigma \left[\rho + \frac{1}{N}(1 - \rho) \right]^{1/2}$ in equation (3.4). This term represents the variability of the firm's cash flow stream in relation to the total assets of the firm $\left\{ \text{that is, } NK\sigma \left[\rho + \frac{1}{N}(1 - \rho) \right]^{1/2} /NK \right\}$. This measure of variability will be referred to as the relative standard deviation of the firm's cash flow.

Table 3–1 illustrates the effect of firm size and the correlation of cash flows on the relative standard deviation of cash flow for the firm when the standard deviation of the productivity of capital is equal to 1. As noted previously, relative variability decreases with firm size and increases as the correlation of subsidary funds flows increases. Table 3–1 also illustrates the concavity of the relationship between relative variability and firm size. Note that the greatest percentage decrease in the relative standard deviation is achieved as the firm goes from being a small firm to a size five times the size of the standard unit in the model. An important implication of table 3–1 is that there should be greater similarity between the capital structures of two firms that have respectively $50 million of assets and $1 billion of assets than between the capital structures of two firms with assets of $10 million and $50 million.

The role of firm size and the correlation between the cash flows of the firm

Table 3–1
Relative Standard Deviation of Cash Flow of a Large Firm

Correlation	Firm Size (N)					
	2	3	5	10	20	∞
1.0	1.0	1.0	1.0	1.0	1.0	1.0
.9	.975	.966	.959	.954	.951	.949
.8	.949	.931	.917	.906	.900	.894
.7	.922	.894	.872	.854	.846	.837
.6	.894	.856	.825	.800	.787	.775
.5	.866	.815	.775	.742	.725	.707
.4	.837	.775	.721	.678	.656	.632

Note: Relative standard deviation $= \left[\rho + \dfrac{1}{N}(1 - \rho) \right]^{1/2}$.

components in determining the firm's optimal debt to total assets ratio is illustrated by table 3–2. Note that when the cash flows of firm components are perfectly correlated, this simple version of the model predicts that all firms choose the same debt to total assets ratio. The table illustrates the fact that the most dramatic effect of firm size on capital structure occurs in the smallest size class (for example, with $\rho = .7$, a firm of size $N = 2$ chooses a capital structure that contains twice as much debt, on a proportional basis, as a firm of size $N = 1$).

The coupon rate on debt is also an important factor in determining the amount of debt in a firm's capital structure. Differentiating the debt to total assets ratio [equation (3.4)] with respect to the coupon rate on debt gives

$$\frac{\partial(D/K)}{\partial r} = \frac{-1}{r^2} \left\{ (\bar{\theta} - \alpha) - t\sigma \left[\rho + \frac{1}{N}(1 - \rho) \right]^{1/2} \right\}. \qquad (3.7)$$

The term in braces must be positive.[4] Consequently.

$$\frac{\partial(D/K)}{\partial r} < 0.$$

Equation (3.7) suggests that as interest rates rise, firms will attempt to reduce their debt to total assets ratio. The increase in the coupon rate increases the tax deductions provided by a given quantity of debt, which reduces the probability that the firm will be able to use its available tax shields fully. Consequently, a firm must reduce the quantity of debt in its capital structure as the coupon rate on debt increases in order to maintain a given level of assurance that all tax shields will be used.

Table 3–2
Effect of Firm Size and Correlation on the Firm's Debt to Total Assets Ratio

ρ	Firm Size									
	1	2	3	4	5	10	20	40	70	100
1.00	.10	.10	.10	.10	.10	.10	.10	.10	.10	.10
.90	.10	.14	.15	.16	.16	.17	.17	.18	.18	.18
.80	.10	.18	.20	.22	.23	.24	.25	.25	.26	.26
.70	.10	.22	.26	.28	.29	.32	.33	.34	.34	.34
.60	.10	.26	.32	.35	.36	.40	.42	.43	.43	.43
.50	.10	.30	.38	.41	.44	.49	.51	.53	.53	.53
.40	.10	.35	.44	.49	.51	.58	.62	.63	.64	.64
.30	.10	.39	.50	.57	.61	.59	.73	.75	.76	.77
.20	.10	.44	.58	.65	.70	.81	.87	.90	.91	.92
.10	.10	.49	.65	.74	.81	.95	1.00	1.00	1.00	1.00
.00	.10	.54	.73	.85	.93	1.00	1.00	1.00	1.00	1.00

Note: $\dfrac{D}{K} = \dfrac{1}{r}\left\{(\bar{\theta} - \alpha) - t\sigma\left[p + \dfrac{1}{N}(1 - \rho)\right]^{1/2}\right\}$

where

$$\bar{\theta} - \alpha = .16$$
$$t = 2$$
$$\sigma = .075$$
$$r = .10$$

Equation (3.7) also predicts an additional source of variation in capital structure that is related to firm size. In general, small firms are unable to issue debt at the same rate of interest as large firms. To the extent that the coupon rate on debt is a decreasing function of firm size, equation (3.7) predicts that large firms will choose a greater debt to total assets ratio than will small firms.

As might be expected, the debt to total assets ratio is a decreasing function of both σ, the standard deviation of the productivity of capital, and t, the level of confidence that all tax shields can be used. An increase in σ relative to the firm's tax shields requires a reduction in the debt to total assets ratio in order to maintain a given level of confidence, t, that the firm's tax shields will be fully used. Conversely, an increase in the desired level of confidence, given the variability of the productivity of capital, requires that total tax shields be reduced by decreasing the amount of debt in the firm's capital structure. To the extent that these parameters differ across firms according to firm size, the model predicts even greater variability in the debt to total assets ratio as the size of the firm varies.

Conclusion

This chapter has examined the relationship between firm size and capital structure. The model that was developed shows that when the cash flows of the components of a large firm are less than perfectly correlated, the cash flows of a large firm will be less variable (in relation to total assets) than will the cash flows of a small firm. This evidence implies that large firms tend to choose a greater debt to total assets ratio than small firms, holding constant the firm's preferred level of assurance (t) that all tax shields will be fully used. The model is consistent with the DeAngelo-Masulis (1980) model in that the debt to total assets ratio is negatively related to the variability of the firm's revenues and the tax shield substitutes for interest expense in the form of depreciation expense. In addition, the model predicts that the use of leverage is negatively related to the coupon rate on a firm's debt.

In chapter 4, the model is extended by considering the role of taxes in determining capital structure. The predictions of this extension are used in an analysis of aggregated tax return data obtained from the IRS *Source Book*. The predictions of the model are explicitly tested in chapter 5 using accounting and financial data from the COMPUSTAT database.

Notes

1. The variance of cash flow for a firm of size N is

$$\text{Var}\left(\sum_{i=1}^{N} \tilde{C}_i\right) = \text{Var}\left(K \sum_{i=1}^{N} \tilde{\theta}_i\right)$$
$$= K^2 \sum_{i=1}^{N} \sigma_i^2 + 2K^2 \sum_{i=1}^{N} \sum_{j=i+1}^{N} \sigma_{ij}$$
$$= K^2[N\sigma^2 + N(N-1)\rho\sigma^2]$$
$$= N^2 K^2 \sigma^2 \left[\rho + \frac{1}{N}(1-\rho)\right].$$

2. This formulation can easily be modified to account for the fact that the cost of borrowing may be a function of firm size.

3. In general, these characteristics may be related to firm size.

4. This follows from the fact that the firm's debt to total assets ratio must be greater than or equal to zero. This point is demonstrated in appendix 3A.

Appendix 3A

Proof that $\dfrac{\partial(D/K)}{\partial r} < 0$

In order for the debt to total assets ratio to decrease as the coupon rate on debt increases, $(\bar{\theta} - \alpha)$ must be greater than $t\sigma \left[\rho + \dfrac{1}{N}(1 - \rho) \right]^{1/2}$.

Note that by assumption,

$$t = \frac{(\bar{\theta} - \alpha) - rD}{\sigma \left[\rho + \dfrac{1}{N}(1 - \rho) \right]^{1/2}} .$$

Consequently, for $D \geqslant 0$,

$$t \leqslant \frac{(\bar{\theta} - \alpha)}{\sigma \left[\rho + \dfrac{1}{N}(1 - \rho) \right]^{1/2}} ,$$

which implies that

$$(\bar{\theta} - \alpha) > t\sigma \left[\rho + \dfrac{1}{N}(1 - \rho) \right]^{1/2} .$$

As a result, $\dfrac{\partial D/K}{\partial r} < 0$.

4

Taxes, Financial Policy, and Firm Size: An Analysis of Internal Revenue Service Data

I n this chapter, IRS *Statistics of Income* data are analyzed to determine the effect of U.S. federal tax policy on firms of different sizes. The principal objectives of the analysis are to determine the extent to which the ability to take tax deductions is a function of firm size and to determine how corporate financial policy with respect to leverage and dividend payout are related to size and taxes.

Internal Revenue Service Data

Data are taken from the *Statistics of Income, Corporation Income Tax Returns* (*SOI*) for the years 1973–1979, which contain data for 11 asset size categories for each of 8 major industrial divisions: agriculture, forestry, and fishing; mining; construction; manufacturing; transportation and public utilities; wholesale and retail trade; finance, insurance, and real estate; and services. The smallest size category contains firms with assets between $0 and $100,000. The largest size category contains firms with assets in excess of $250 million.

In addition, the *Corporation Source Book* data tape was analyzed for the year 1976, the latest year for which these data were publicly available. The *Source Book* contains a more complete industry breakdown than the *SOI* and presents more data for each industry and size class than are available in the *SOI*. (See appendix 4A, beginning on p. 69, for tables mentioned in this chapter.)

Major Features of Corporate Taxation

Three aspects of the federal tax code affect a corporation's tax bill: (1) the statutory tax rate, (2) the deductions allowed in arriving at taxable income, and (3) the tax credits permitted to reduce the tax bill.

Statutory Tax Rate

Table 4A–1 presents the statutory marginal corporate tax rates in the period 1973–1980. As is evident in the table, only minor changes in corporate tax rates have come into effect during this period. The most important change occurred in 1979 when the progressivity of the tax rate was increased and the maximum marginal tax rate reduced from 48 percent to 46 percent.

Allowable Deductions

In recent years major changes in corporate tax obligations have been brought about not so much by changing what may be deducted but by changing the timing of deductions. For example, allowing an expenditure to be expensed rather than depreciated or depreciated at an accelerated pace can significantly reduce a firm's tax bill. The Economic Recovery Tax Act of 1981 made major modifications in the tax code to increase the rate at which capital equipment may be depreciated. While IRS data are not available for this more recent period, the analysis of earlier years provides evidence of the relative benefits to large and small firms of such changes in the tax law.

Tax Credits

The major tax credits available to corporations during the period of this study are the investment tax credit and the foreign tax credit (of minor importance are the work incentive credit and the possession tax credit). The Tax Reduction Act of 1975 increased the investment tax credit from 7 percent of "investment qualified for credit" to 10 percent and broadened the property eligible for the credit. For investment with a life of 3 to 5 years, one-third of the "cost of property used for the investment credit" was "investment qualified for credit." For investments with a life of 5 to 7 years, two-thirds of the cost qualified for credit. One hundred percent of the cost of investments with a life of more than 7 years was qualified for the credit. Certain limitations on this credit applied. In particular, the credit was limited to 50 percent of any tax obligation over $25,000. After 1978 the 50 percent limitation was relaxed by 10 percentage points per year until 1982 when a credit could be taken against 90 percent of the tax liability over $25,000. Any unused credit can be carried back 3 years or forward 7 years. The foreign tax credit is of considerable significance for large corporations but is relatively unimportant for small corporations.

Certain corporations—small business corporations—are not taxed directly but pass income (or loss) directly through to their shareholders, who pay tax as individuals. Election of small business corporation status is limited to corporations with relatively few shareholders (15 during the period of our analysis) and

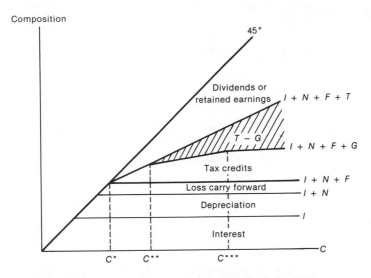

Figure 4–1. Composition of Corporation's Cash Flow

is subject to a number of other restrictions. Small business corporations file Form 1120S, and most of the information for these firms is included in the *SOI* and *Source Book* data. However, there is no tax liability for these corporations since all taxes are paid by the individual owners.

Composition of Corporate Cash Flow and Taxes

The business activities of a corporation generate a cash flow, C, before interest and taxes. This cash flow may be used for capital investments to replace deteriorating plants or to expand and to make payments to the claimants on the firm's earnings—the government (taxes, T), the bondholders (interest, I), and the stockholders (dividends, D). Taxable income is realized only if C exceeds the sum of interest (I), depreciation and other noncash charges (N), and net operating loss carry forward (F) from prior years. The composition of cash flow and certain critical levels of C are illustrated in figure 4–1.

The relationship between the corporation's tax liability before credits and its cash flow is examined first. We then turn to a consideration of tax credits.

The corporation's tax liability before tax credits is given as

$$\tilde{T} = t_c(\tilde{C} - N - I - F) \qquad \text{for } \tilde{C} > C^*,$$
$$= 0 \qquad \text{for } \tilde{C} < C^*,$$

where

$\bar{T}$ = corporation's dollar tax liability before credits, a random variable;
$\tilde{C}$ = random cash flow before interest and taxes;
N = depreciation and other noncash charges, assumed to be nonrandom;
I = interest charges;
F = loss carry forward from prior years, assumed to be nonrandom;
t_c = statutory corporate tax rate;
C^* = $N + I + F$, the critical level of cash flow below which some tax deductions are wasted.

The greater the probability that $\tilde{C} < C^*$, the lower the benefit of additional tax deductions in the form of interest expense or depreciation expense. This statement can be formalized by deriving the marginal benefit of additional interest deductions.

The expected tax liability is given as

$$E(\bar{T}) = \int_{C^*}^{\infty} (\tilde{C} - N - I - F)t_c f(C)dC,$$

where $f(C)$ is the probability distribution of C. The marginal effective expected tax benefit of additional interest deductions is then given as

$$\frac{\partial E(T)}{\partial I} = -t_c^* = -t_c \int_{C^*}^{\infty} f(C)dC,$$

where t_c^* is the marginal effective tax rate. The benefit of additional interest deductions is thus simply the negative of the statutory tax rate times the probability of having sufficient income to use the additional interest deduction. We shall use the IRS data to estimate t_c^* for small and large firms.

The IRS data also lend themselves to the calculation of alternative measures of average effective tax rates. An average effective tax rate is the expected tax payment divided by a measure of expected income or cash flow. Four alternative measures are listed now along with the variable names of the empirical proxies to be calculated from the IRS data:

$$1. \quad \frac{E(T)}{\int_{C^* - F}^{\infty} (\tilde{C} - N - I - F)f(C)dC} = \frac{T}{YT}$$

$$2. \quad \frac{E(T)}{E(C) - N - I} = \frac{T}{\Pi}$$

$$3.\ \frac{E(T)}{\displaystyle\int_{C^* - F}^{\infty} (\bar{C} - N - I)f(C)dC} = \frac{T}{Y}$$

$$4.\ \frac{E(T)}{E(C)} = \frac{T}{CBIT}$$

In the empirical work, expectations are taken cross sectionally within asset size. This assumes that the cross-sectional distribution of C is comparable to the distribution of C for an individual firm, an assumption that is realistic, particularly when the data are also classified by industry. Different measures of average effective tax rates may be calculated because the data distinguish firms with income $(C > C^* - F)$ from firms with losses $(C < C^* - F)$. Note that the IRS classification is based on net income, not on taxable income. Net income does not reflect any loss carry forwards.[1] Thus, the first ratio is the expected tax liability of all firms in a class divided by expected taxable income of the firms in the class that have positive net income $(C > C^* - F)$. The ratio, $\frac{T}{YT}$, is a good estimate of the statutory tax rate in each size class since the denominator is taxable income after loss carry forwards and other statutory special deductions.

The second ratio divides the tax liability by the net income of all firms— averaging in firms with losses. This ratio, $\frac{T}{\Pi}$, measures the overall tax liability of all firms in the class and is expected to exceed the statutory tax rate because firms with losses reduce the denominator of the fraction while they do not affect the numerator. While losses of firms with losses are reflected in the denominator, loss carry forwards of profitable firms are not.

The third measure, $\frac{T}{Y}$, divides the tax liability by net income of firms with income. This measure understates the average tax ratio since the tax liability is divided by a measure of income that omits loss carry forwards or current losses by firms with losses.

The fourth measure, $\frac{T}{CBIT}$, divides by cash flow before interest and taxes (CBIT) on the grounds that CBIT is a better measure of the firm's true earnings. This is because depreciation for tax purposes, N, may overstate economic depreciation and because one frequently measures income to the firm prior to interest expenses. The higher value of the denominator is likely to cause this measure of the average effective tax rate to be considerably lower than some of the other measures.

We now turn to the relationship of cash flow, C, and tax credits, G. Tax credits—principally the investment tax credit (ITC) and the foreign tax credit— reduce the tax liability of a corporation up to a limit. Two critical points, C^{**}

and C^{***}, related to tax credits are illustrated in figure 4–1. For values of $\bar{C}$ between C^* and C^{**}, the tax liability is wholly offset by tax credits. This occurs, for example, if $T < 25,000$ and $ITC > 25,000$. For values of $\bar{C}$ between C^{**} and C^{***}, the tax liability is only partially offset by tax credits because the investment tax credit could be used to offset only a fraction of the tax liability in excess of \$25,000. Only if $C > C^{***}$ does the corporation pay the full statutory tax rate on income, since C^{***} is the point beyond which the tax credit has been used up.

In figure 4–1, the shaded area labeled $T - G$ is the actual corporate tax payment. The remainder of $\bar{C}$ is available to pay interest, to pay dividends, or to reinvest in additional assets.

In the empirical analysis that follows, we examine whether small firms have more variable cash flow streams than large firms and consider the relative tax benefits for small and for large firms of further deductions from income. The following hypotheses are considered:

1. The variability of income and cash flow is greater for small firms than for large firms.
2. The benefit of additional tax deductions as measured by alternative measures of effective tax rates and by the use of available tax credits is lower for small firms than for large firms. This is due to the variability of small firms' cash flows and possibly to the greater level of depreciation and interest expense relative to average CBIT.

We shall also examine the size pattern of debt-equity ratios and interest expense and carry out regression analysis of the relationship between debt levels and tax variables and certain other factors. Finally, the chapter contains sections on dividend policy as related to firm size and certain other factors.

Variability of Income by Size of Firm

Two measures of the variability of income by size of firm can be obtained from the *SOI*. The first, the ratio of the number of returns with net income to the total number of returns of active corporations, is given in table 4A–2 for the aggregate of all industries for the years 1973–1979. Net income is defined as gross taxable receipts less ordinary and necessary business deductions including depreciation and interest expense. For the very smallest firms with positive assets between \$1 and \$100,000, the ratio is slightly above .50. The ratio rises to the neighborhood of .7 for the next size class and then continues to rise slowly with increases in size. It is evident from these data that a greater proportion of small firms than large firms suffer losses. Part of the phenomenon is undoubtedly due to the fact that certain firms are small because they are unprofitable and are in the process of going out of business. But part of the phenomenon reflects the fact that small firms, while profitable on average, are more likely to incur a loss in any given year.

A second ratio takes account of the dollar magnitude of profits and losses and is available by major industrial division as well as by asset size. This ratio is calculated as $Y/(Y + L)$, where

Y = net income of firms with income,
L = losses of firms with losses.[2]

This measure is thus an alternative indication of the probability that a firm in a given size class will have income against which to take tax deductions.

Table 4A–3 presents data for all industries for the years 1973–1979, and table 4A–4 presents data for selected industries and asset sizes. The numbers in table 4A–3 correspond quite closely to those in table 4A–2, indicating the greater probability of losses among small firms. For the largest size category the ratio, $Y/(Y + L)$, in table 4A–3 exceeds the ratio of profitable firms to all firms in table 4A–2. This suggests that the losses of those firms with losses in the largest size category were small compared to the profits of those firms with profits. The data in table 4A–4 indicate that the greater tendency for losses in the small size category is consistent across industries.

A third measure of variability is available from the *Source Book* for 1976. This measure is the net operating loss carry forward taken as a fraction of net income of non-1120S corporations with income. The greater the frequency of losses in prior years, the larger this ratio. The data in table 4A–5 indicate that, except in agriculture, the ratio declines with asset size.

On the basis of the three ratios just examined, one can conclude that the variability of income is greater for small firms than for large firms and that small firms are more likely to be in a loss situation and unable to utilize all available tax deductions.

Effective Tax Rates before Tax Credits

In the calculation of effective tax rates from IRS, *SOI*, and *Source Book* data, two measures of tax obligations and four measures of income are used. These measures are first defined. This section then presents some data on marginal and average effective tax rates, with an emphasis on tax rates before tax credits. Succeeding sections examine the investment tax credit and foreign tax credit.

Two measures of the tax obligations are considered:

T = tax liability before tax credits,
$T - G$ = tax liability after tax credits,

where G = investment tax credit plus the foreign tax credit plus certain other minor tax credits.

Four measures of income are considered:

Y = before-tax net income of corporations with income;

YT = taxable income of corporations with income. YT differs from Y by the amount of certain statutory special deductions that include the net operating loss (NOL) carry forward from prior years and the intercorporate dividend payment deduction;[3]

Π = net income of firms with income less deficit of firms with deficit;

$CBIT$ = cash flow before interest and taxes. Calculated as $CBIT = \Pi + I + N$, where I = interest paid and N = depreciation. The *SOI* data report only gross interest expense. The *Source Book* data (available for 1976) permit calculation of interest expense net of interest income, and when *Source Book* data are used, $CBIT$ is calculated on the basis of net interest expense. Use of gross interest expense biases $CBIT$ upward in the finance and real estate industry since firms in these industries have substantial offsetting interest income. This bias carries over to the aggregate of all industries. As a result, analysis of *SOI* data involving $CBIT$ should be carried out within industrial divisions.

While the two measures of taxes and four measures of income give eight possible ratios, data on five ratios are presented. The five ratios and their expected relationship to each other are as follows:

$$\frac{T - G}{CBIT} < \frac{T}{CBIT} < \frac{T}{Y} < \frac{T}{YT} < \frac{T}{\Pi}.$$

Data for these ratios for all industries and for those industrial divisions— manufacturing, wholesale and retail trade, and services—are presented in tables 4A–6 to 4A–9 for three asset size categories and for the years 1973 to 1979. Data for the smallest available asset size category (0–$100,000) are not reported in these tables because this size category is likely to contain many transitory firms in the process of ceasing operations, the data for which are likely to be unrepresentative for ongoing small firms in that class.

Three patterns are evident in the data. First, the different ratios tend to have the expected relationship to each other. Second, the value of each ratio tends to be smallest for the small size category. Third, the ratios tend to decline over time. Each of these patterns is now discussed with respect to the data for manufacturing in table 4A–7. Data for other industries reflect similar patterns.

For any year and within a size class, the pattern of ratios is as expected.

While the estimate of the statutory tax rate in the small asset size is $\frac{T}{YT} = .1981$ in 1979, tax liability as a fraction of overall income in the class, netting out losses, is higher—$\frac{T}{\Pi} = .2569$—as expected. Larger measures of income—Y, CBIT—yield correspondingly smaller measures of tax rates. Only in the largest size class is it the case that $\frac{T}{\Pi} < \frac{T}{YT}$. This is due to the fact that subtracting statutory special deductions (loss carry forwards and intercorporate dividends) from net income of firms with income (in arriving at YT) reduces the divisor by more than subtracting the losses of firms with losses (in arriving at Π). It is also interesting to note the substantial decline in 1979 from $T/CBIT$ to $(T - G)/CBIT$ for the smallest and largest firms.

The size pattern of each tax ratio is not entirely as expected. It is the case that each ratio is smallest in the smallest size category, usually substantially so. However, certain tax ratios have a humped pattern with respect to size. In particular, tax payments after credits decline as a fraction of *CBIT* for the largest firms. This phenomenon is discussed later as part of the analysis of the foreign tax credit. And when the pattern is not humped, tax rates rise and then flatten out after a certain asset size.

Of considerable interest is the decline over time in tax rates, a decline that appears to be more pronounced among small firms than among large firms. The decline appears to be the result of reductions in statutory tax rates (see table 4A–1) and perhaps increased deductions for interest expense in a period of rising interest rates.

As indicated earlier, there is a possible bias in some of the tax ratios because of the presence of 1120S corporations that pay no tax but that have income that is included in some of the measures of income (namely, in Y, Π, and *CBIT* although not in YT since 1120S firms have no taxable income). Table 4A–10 contains data for the ratios $\frac{T}{Y'}$ and $\frac{T}{\Pi'}$, where Y' is net income of firms with income excluding net income of 1120S firms and Π' is net income less deficit of all corporations except 1120S corporations. The adjustment raises the ratios for small corporations relative to large corporations; however, the basic patterns discussed earlier are maintained.

The average effective tax rates indicate clearly that the benefits of additional tax deductions, whether in the form of interest expense or accelerated depreciation, are less for small firms than for large firms. This is due primarily to the lower statutory tax rate of small firms and in part to the higher probability that small firms will not have sufficient income to take tax deductions.

A clearer picture of the relative importance of the statutory rate and of the probability of income is given in table 4A–11, which contains estimates of marginal expected effective tax rates for certain industries and three asset size categories for the years 1973–1979. These estimates are calculated as

$$t^* = t_c \int_{C^* - F}^{\infty} f(C)dC,$$

where t_c is given by $\dfrac{T}{YT}$ and the integral is approximated by $\dfrac{Y}{Y + L}$ from tables 4A–3 and 4A–4. Note that the ratio, $\dfrac{Y}{Y + L}$, is the income before loss carry forwards of firms with income relative to the sum of net income and deficit. There is a greater probability that $C > C^* - F$ than that $C > C^*$. As a result, effective tax rates are somewhat overstated. Of course, our estimates also depend crucially on the degree to which the ratio, $\dfrac{Y}{Y + L}$, reflects the probability of income in each size class. Our measure of effective tax rates is an understatement to the extent that firms with losses can carry losses forward to future years in which income is available and tax savings may be generated.

For 1979, manufacturing firms with assets between $100,000 and $250,000 have a marginal effective tax rate of 13.96 percent as compared with a statutory rate of 19.81 percent. In the largest size category of manufacturing firms, the marginal effective rate is 43.84 percent as compared with a statutory rate of 45.05 percent. This means that the expected marginal benefits of another dollar of tax deductions (such as interest expense) in only 14¢ for the small manufacturing firms while it is 44¢ for the large manufacturing firms. That small firms have lower effective tax rates than large firms is common to all industries and so is the fact that there is a greater gap between the effective and statutory rate for small firms than large. It is thus clear that the tax benefits of interest deductions of further acceleration of depreciation are much less for small firms than large. The existence of tax credits further reduces marginal effective tax rates and the benefits of tax deductions.

Investment Tax Credit

It is evident from the comparison of *T/CBIT* and *(T − G)/CBIT* in tables 4A–6 to 4A–9 that tax credits reduced the tax bill of corporations, particularly in 1978 and 1979. In this section the investment tax credit is examined from two perspectives: first, to gain an understanding of the relative magnitude of the credit for small and large firms and, second, to assess the extent to which utilization of the credit is limited because the firm is in the range below C^{***} in figure 4–1. The next section examines the foreign tax credit.

Some terms are first defined, and the 1976 *Source Book* line number is given where appropriate:

P_1: Cost of property used for investment credit (*Source Book* line 90).

P_2: Investment qualified for credit (*Source Book* line 91). Only a fraction of the cost of property used for investment credit is investment qualified for credit. The fraction depends on the property's life as follows:

3–5 years of life: One-third of cost qualified,
5–7 years of life: Two-thirds of cost qualified,
7^+ years of life: 100 percent of cost qualifed.

The definition of investment qualified for credit was changed substantially in 1981 with the introduction of the accelerated cost recovery system (ACRS) of depreciation.

TITC: Tentative investment credit (*Source Book* line 92) = $P_2 k$, where k = investment tax credit rate, usually .10.

ITCO: Investment credit carry over (*Source Book* line 93). Investment credits carried over from prior years; for most of the period, the investment credit could not be claimed to the extent it exceeded $25,000 of income tax plus 50 percent of the tax in excess of $25,000. Higher limits applied after 1976.

TTC: Total tentative credit = $TITC + ITCO$.

ITC: Investment tax credit (*Source Book* line 84). Actual investment credit taken in a particular year; may include investment credit carry over; $ITC \leq TTC$.

Although the comparison of $T/CBIT$ and $(T - G)/CBIT$ implies that the investment tax credit is of considerable importance to small firms, the credit is a smaller fraction of the cost of property used for investment credit in the case of small firms than it is in the case of large firms. This is reflected in the ratio, $\dfrac{ITC}{P_1}$, presented in table 4A–12 for the aggregate of all industries. Two explanations are possible for the size trend evident in table 4A–12. First, small firms may purchase property with a shorter life than large firms. This would reduce the allowable investment credit relative to the cost of the property. Second, small corporations may be unable to claim the full credit because of inadequate incomes and therefore inadequate taxes against which to claim the credit. The *Source Book* for 1976 provides sufficient data to examine these explanations, but there are insufficient data in the *SOI* to carry out a more detailed analysis for the other years.

The fact that small firms purchase shorter-lived property is reflected in table 4A–13, which indicates that qualified investment as a fraction of the cost of investment credit property (P_2/P_1) increases with asset size. Because of this factor, small firms are able to qualify a smaller fraction of capital expenditures than large firms. Furthermore, since small firms are less capital intensive than large firms, they purchase less investment property of any life than large firms.

Despite the fact that small firms are less capital intensive and benefit less from the investment tax credit, they use a smaller fraction of the tentative credit than large firms. Even for the largest firm, the ratio, *ITC/TTC*, shown in table 4A–13, is surprisingly small. For example, in 1976 manufacturing firms with assets between $100,000 and $250,000 used only 50 percent of the available investment tax credit. In the largest size category, 74 percent of the tentative credit was used. This is consistent with the earlier finding that small firms are more likely to incur losses than large firms and implies that small firms are less able than large firms to take advantage of existing tax deductions.

Foreign Tax Credit

U.S. multinational corporations producing income in foreign countries receive a credit for income tax paid to foreign governments. For example, a U.S. corporation generating net income of $100 in a foreign country that has a tax rate of 30 percent would pay $30 of tax abroad. When the remaining profit of $70 is repatriated to the United States, U.S. "grossed-up" income of $70/(1 − 0.3) = $100 is reported, and a tax liability of $46 is calculated (assuming a U.S. tax rate of 0.46). However, a foreign tax credit of $30 is given to offset this tax liability since $30 of taxes have already been paid to the foreign government. The final U.S. tax liability is thus $16.

Data on the foreign tax credit as a fraction of CBIT are presented in table 4A–14. This ratio is significantly higher for the largest size class than for all other size classes because multinational corporations tend to be the largest of U.S. corporations. The large foreign tax credit thus explains the dramatic drop from *T/CBIT* to $(T − G)/CBIT$ observed earlier in the largest size class. The economic significance of this drop should not, however, be overstated. The size of the foreign tax credit simply reflects the size of taxes already paid to foreign governments. The greater the foreign income of a U.S. corporation, the larger will be the foreign tax credit as a fraction of CBIT. Thus, the foreign tax credit is quite different from the investment tax credit that is an additional tax benefit.

Profitability and Size

While the relationship between profitability and size is not the focus of this book, we are interested in examining a particular measure of profits, CBIT, that we use as a standard against which other flow variables such as taxes, interest, depreciation, and dividends are measured. CBIT is viewed as exogenous to the financial decisions of the firm. We examine two measures of profitability—*CBIT/TA, CBIT/TR*, where *TA* = total assets and *TR* = total receipts—to determine if *CBIT* is stable in the sense that no economic forces exist to cause it to change. For example, a value of *CBIT/TA* = 0 is not stable. Firms would tend to leave this industry and size class until a sustainable profitability is achieved. *CBIT* would not, in this case, be an exogenous standard against which to measure other variables of interest.

Value of the ratios, *CBIT/TA, CBIT/TR*, are given in tables 4A–15 and 4A–16. As expected, *CBIT/TR* increases dramatically with firm size. This trend reflects the lower operating margin of small firms as compared with large firms, which tends to be offset by the higher sales to assets turnover among small firms. Within each size category, there is substantial stability over time.

If one is concerned to measure profitability, the most appropriate deflator for CBIT is total assets. Total assets are preferred to total receipts because total assets represent the investment made by stockholders and bondholders who have a claim on CBIT. Total assets are preferred to equity as a deflator since CBIT includes interest. For this measure of profitability, there is not evidence of a very strong size pattern, as in the case of *CBIT/TR*. In manufacturing, there is some evidence of a humped pattern while, in services, there appears to be a decline with size.[4] However, these patterns are not as strong as the increase in profitability over time (due perhaps to inflation). If profit ratios are calculated for firms with income, there is a decline in profitability with increases in size. This is due to the fact that losses are more common among small firms. The measure in table 4A–16 is appropriate because firms are concerned with average profits over good and bad years. On the basis of the data in tables 4A–15 and 4A–16 there is no reason to question the appropriateness of *CBIT* as a standard or deflator for other flow variables.

Depreciation

The probability that cash flow will be too small to utilize all available tax deductions depends not only on the volatility of cash flow but also on the size of existing tax deductions. The greater the existing tax deductions, the less the probability they can all be used. Data on the magnitude of an important tax deduction—depreciation—are presented in table 4A–17.

The data indicate that depreciation is a larger fraction of CBIT for small firms than for large firms. (Only in the service industry is this size trend not evident.) For example, in 1979, depreciation was 38.57 percent of CBIT for manufacturing firms with assets between $100,000 and $250,000 while it was only 24.59 percent for the largest size class. This is surprising because capital intensity is thought to be lower the smaller the firm. The explanation appears to be that small firms acquire assets of shorter life, something that was reflected in the ratio of investment tax credit to cost of investment credit property calculated earlier. Since such assets may be depreciated more rapidly, depreciation expense as a fraction of CBIT is larger for small firms. While the higher depreciation expense of small firms is beneficial to them in reducing taxes, it also implies that additional tax deductions, in the form of interest payments, for example, are less valuable to small firms.

Interest Expense

Interest expense, more than depreciation, is under the control of the firm. The desired level of debt depends on a variety of factors, many of which were discussed in chapter 1, and on taxes. Holding constant other factors, the greater the probability of not having sufficient income to take tax deductions, the lower the desired level of debt. A model of capital structure choice based on this principle was presented earlier. An alternate view is that the observed level of debt may reflect the fact that a corporation is forced by circumstances to an unwanted level of debt where the probability of realizing tax benefits is reduced.

In examining interest expense, the purpose is not to test theories of the capital structure. We have a more modest objective of examining the magnitude of interest deductions as a function of firm size without an attempt to test the relationship between capital structure and taxes. Such tests are carried out later.

Table 4A–18 contains data on the fraction of CBIT paid out in the form of interest. Because gross interest expense before netting out interest income is used in table 4A–18, the data are somewhat misleading. This is particularly so in the all-industries category that includes financial corporations. The problem is less in manufacturing, trades, and services but does exist, as a comparison of tables 4A–18 and 4A–19 suggests. For 1976, net interest data are available (from the *Source Book*) and are presented in table 4A–19. It is evident from table 4A–19 that large firms have greater interest income than small firms. Indeed, the negative net interest expense of large financial corporations causes net interest for all large corporations to be negative.

Consistent size patterns are difficult to detect in tables 4A–18 and 4A–19. Gross interest as a fraction of CBIT tends to increase with firm size in trade and services. In manufacturing there is greater tendency for decreases with firm size. These patterns are not maintained when net interest is examined, at least in 1976. Net interest of all firms (income and loss firms) declines with firm size in manufacturing and trade. A humped pattern exists in services. When consideration is restricted to firms with income, there is no size trend in the ratio, *I/CBIT*, except in services for which the humped pattern is maintained. The data suggest that small firms (in manufacturing and services) choose debt levels comparable to large firms on the assumption of having income. The existence of losses thus raises the ratio of interest paid to average cash flow. Using average cash flow as a deflator is correct, however, since small firms do run losses and are, in those cases, less able to make interest payments.

The apparent high interest expense of small firms reflected in tables 4A–18 and 4A–19 is surprising is view of the relatively lower tax benefits small firms derive from interest deductions. A possible explanation is that the high cost of the alternative—equity financing—leaves small firms no choice.

Financial Policy

Leverage Ratios

Several factors discussed in chapter 1—agency costs, information costs, transaction costs—suggest that small firms would tend to be more heavily levered than large firms, ceteris paribus. Furthermore, small firms would be expected to have a higher ratio of short-term debt to long-term debt since monitoring of management is facilitated by such a financing pattern. In contrast, the fact that small firms have greater difficulty in realizing the tax benefits of debt implies that small firms would be less levered than large. These offsetting factors, as well as other compounding factors related to industry, capital intensity, and income variability, make it difficult to predict the relative degree of leverage of small and large corporations.

Tax factors have no particular implication for the ratio of short-term to long-term debt. As a result, one would expect, on the basis of the theory in chapter 1, relatively higher levels of short-term debt for small firms than for large.

Two measures of leverage are calculated from the *SOI* data for the years 1973–1979 for certain industries and asset sizes: the ratio of the book value of total assets to the book value of equity (table 4A–20) and the ratio of the book value of total assets less current liabilities to the book value of equity (table 4A–21). The second measure is a ratio of all long-term financing—long-term debt, other liabilities including loans from stockholders, and equity—to equity. In manufacturing, small firms tend to be somewhat more highly levered than large firms. In services there is a humped pattern—middle-sized firms have higher leverage than small or large firms. In trade, there is no size trend in leverage. These data are not consistent with a theory of capital structure based solely on taxes since small firms frequently have higher levels of debt than large firms, despite the lower tax rate of small firms. The data are consistent with the view that the natural tendency toward higher leverage on the part of small firms is partly offset by the lower tax benefits of leverage to small firms.

One characteristic of small firms worth noting is the much greater importance of loans to and from stockholders. For example, for firms with $100,000 to $250,000 of assets, loans from stockholders as a percentage of total assets ranged between 6.9 and 9.7 percent in the years 1973–1979. Loans to stockholders ranged between 1.67 and 3.06 percent for this size class. Data for the five smallest asset size categories for all industries are contained in table 4A–22. Exclusion of these loans from the measures of leverage, on the grounds that stockholder loans are equity, would reduce the leverage of small firms in tables 4A–20 and 4A–21.[5]

The ratio of current liabilities to long-term debt was calculated as a measure of the maturity structure of debt (table 4A–23). The data do not support the theoretical conjecture that short-term liabilities would decline as a fraction of long-term liabilities as firm size increases. In manufacturing, there is a tendency for the largest firms to have a lower level of short-term to long-term debt as compared with small firms. In trade, there is a humped pattern, and in services there is a U-shaped pattern. The lack of a consistent size pattern suggests that other factors may be related to size that influence the maturity structure of liabilities and that overwhelm the pattern of financing that might be optimal from the perspective of monitoring managers. In particular, customs with respect to the extension of trade credit may be responsible for the observed patterns.

Leverage Regressions

Theoretical arguments made earlier suggest that financial leverage should be positively related to a corporation's effective tax rate and negatively related to the level of depreciation expense. The higher the effective tax rate, the greater the tax benefit of interest deductions. Similarly, the greater depreciation expense, the lower the probability that interest deductions can be taken. A wide range of other factors also affects the leverage decision. These include the factors discussed in chapter 1 that are related to the optimal financial structure for monitoring managers as well as institutional factors related to a particular industry.

A further complication arises from the fact that theories of capital structure specify an equilibrium capital structure. Data, in contrast, are available only for particular years. The IRS data, by grouping firms, makes it impossible to average over time data for a particular firm or otherwise conduct tests to determine if the firm is at its desired debt level. There is thus the danger that firms with high debt are only temporarily in that position. There is also the danger that effective tax rates contain a transitory element.

Despite these difficulties one would, nevertheless, expect the hypothesized relationship to be evident in the data. This expectation was not confirmed by the data.

While we used alternative measures of leverage and alternative combinations of independent variables, the following regression is representative:

$$\frac{B^1}{TA} = a_0 + a_1 t^* + a_2 \frac{N}{TA} + a_3 S,$$

where

B^1 = long-term debt less net loans from stockholders;

TA = total assets;

t^* = effective tax rate defined as $\dfrac{Y}{Y+L}$ (T/YT);

N = the sum of depreciation, amortization, and depletion;

S = the size category, a number between 1 and 10, where 1 refers to the smallest size category used—$100,000 to $250,000 in assets—and 10 refers to the largest category—$250 million or more in assets. The smallest available asset size—$1 to $100,000—was not used because of the many transitional firms in this category.

Using *Source Book* data for 1976, the regression was run across 10 size categories and all four-digit industries within each of three major industrial divisions—manufacturing, wholesale and retail trade (trade), and services. The results are summarized in table 4A–24. Results for alternative specifications were similar.

The most surprising result in table 4A–24, one we do not fully understand, is the significant negative coefficient on the effective tax rate. According to this coefficient, the higher the effective tax rate, the lower the level of long-term debt. The significant negative coefficient for the effective tax rate is unchanged if total debt—including short-term debt—is used as the dependent variable. A possible explanation of this result is that those groups of firms with low effective tax rates are in financial difficulty [that is, have low values of $Y/(Y+L)$] and are compelled to borrow in excess of their desired debt level. The narrower the industry division, the more likely is it that all the firms in a particular asset size category will be subject to the same economic forces, and therefore, the more likely is it that all firms in a particular size category are subject to abnormal financial difficulty while other size categories may experience exceptional profits.

Also surprising is the positive coefficient for the depreciation variable, N/TA. This implies that debt level is positively related to depreciation expense. While this result is contrary to our tax-effect hypothesis, there may be a plausible alternative explanation. In particular, the ratio, N/TA, may be a measure of collateral value of corporate assets—higher depreciation expense, suggesting the existence of a greater number of tangible (and repossessable) assets. Firms with higher tangible assets may qualify for a greater level of debt. When the leverage ratio is calculated using total debt (including short-term liabilities), the importance of the depreciation variable in the regression is reduced in the case of manufacturing and trade. This implies that long-term lending rather than short-term lending is related to depreciation levels.

The coefficient of the size variable is positive, which implies that large firms are more levered than small firms, holding constant effective tax rates and depreciation. This result is also puzzling since one would expect large firms to be more levered than small firms because of the tax effect, not in spite of it, as these results imply.

In summary, we are left with some puzzling regression results that deserve further analysis. While the relation of leverage to depreciation has sensible explanations, the relation of leverage to effective tax rates and to size is a puzzle. There may be interaction effects among the variables to explain the results, or as suggested earlier, firms in transition may explain the results.

Dividends

Corporations acting in the interest of shareholders maximize the permanent, long-run, level of operating cash flow after interest, taxes, and needed expenditure to maintain plant and equipment, holding constant the level of risk to shareholders. The remaining cash flow is paid out to shareholders or reinvested in additional plant and equipment if the firm has investment opportunities returning more than the cost of capital. Because of the costs of raising outside funds, firms with investment opportunites would be expected to make smaller payments to stockholders.

How cash payments are made to stockholders is also, at least in part, a decision variable for the firm. Cash dividends are taxed twice—once to the corporation, since there is no tax deduction for dividends as there is for interest, and once to the shareholders. An alternative to paying a cash dividend is the repurchase of shares. By selling shares back to the corporation, stockholders have the opportunity to receive capital gains tax treatment. Finally, for small, closely held corporations there may be opportunities to compensate shareholders through other means such as higher salary, various perquisites, and more generous employee benefits for owner-managers.

Data on cash dividends as a fraction of CBIT are presented in table 4A–25 for certain industries and size classes. In manufacturing and trade, there is a reasonably consistent trend for dividends to increase with firm size, although the increase comes primarily in the largest asset size category that contains publicly held firms. In services, there is no clear size pattern.[6] The greater dividend payout of large firms in manufacturing and trade is consistent with either or both of two hypotheses:

1. Small firms have greater investment opportunities and face higher costs of outside financing than large firms. As a result, they retain a greater fraction of earnings.
2. Small firms have alternative methods for paying out profits, such as share repurchase or higher salaries and benefits, to owner-managers.

Data on stock repurchases are not directly available. The *SOI* does contain data on the cost of Treasury stock by asset size category for the aggregate of all industries. For an individual firm, a change in Treasury stock would measure the net repurchases by the firm. However, a change in Treasury stock for a size class reflects the changing composition of the size class as well. Nevertheless, the *SOI* data suggest that increases in Treasury stock have been greater for large corporations than for small corporations. For example, in the period 1975 to 1979, Treasury stock increased from $20.77 billion to $43.89 billion for all firms, while it increased from $6.72 billion to $21.5 billion for the largest size category of firms (assets in excess of $250 million). From 1978 to 1979, Treasury stock of the largest corporations increased from $12.3 billion to $21.5 billion (a change of 0.795 percent of 1979 equity), while all remaining corporations experienced an increase from $19.8 billion to $22.3 billion (a change of 0.463 percent of 1979 equity). One cannot conclude from these data that small firms make greater use than large of share repurchases as an alternative to dividends.

The 1976 *Source Book* data may be used to make calculations on two additional methods for paying out profits: (1) employee benefits and (2) excess officer compensation. These calculations are in table 4A–26 along with the dividend payout. (The dividend payout in table 4A–26 differs from that in table 4A–25 because CBIT is calculated using net interest and including noncash charges of amortization and depletion in addition to depreciation). Employee benefits as a fraction of total receipts tend to increase with company size in all industries except services. This implies that employee benefits are not used by small firms as a substitute for dividends, except perhaps in the service industry.

The flexibility that small closely held corporations have in compensating owners with salary instead of with dividends has long been recognized. Alexander (1949) argued that profitable small firms would increase salary payments to officers to reduce the corporate tax bill. This would be particularly desirable if the individual tax rate were less than the corporate rate. The alternative to paying excess salary would be to pay dividends or to retain earnings for later payout. Dividend payments would, however, be subject to individual tax. Deferral would postpone individual tax and may be desirable when the individual tax exceeds the corporate tax. Alexander argued that firms without income had no incentive to overpay officers since corporate taxes were already zero for these firms. Thus, he calculated excess officer compensations as the amount by which actual officers' salaries in profitable firms exceeded predicted officers' salaries in profitable firms, where the prediction is based on the ratio of officer salaries to assets of unprofitable firms.

We make a similar calculation using total receipts rather than total assets. We calculate

$$EC = O_P - \frac{O_L}{TR_L} TR_P,$$

where

$$EC = \text{excess compensation,}$$
$$O_P = \text{officer salaries in profitable firms,}$$
$$O_L = \text{officer salaries in loss firms,}$$
$$TR_L, TR_P = \text{total receipts of loss and profitable firms respectively.}$$

Table 4A–26 reports that the ratio, $EC/CBIT$, declines dramatically with asset size, which suggests that there is a tendency for small profitable firms to pay some of their profits in the form of salary. The ratio undoubtedly overstates the magnitude of this effect since owner-managers in companies with losses may reduce salaries. Nevertheless, the evidence is not inconsistent with the hypothesis that small firms use salaries as a way of paying out profits.

An alternative explanation for a low dividend payout is the existence of internal investment opportunities at a return exceeding stockholder alternatives if funds are paid out. Data on the cost of investment tax credit property as a fraction of CBIT (table 4A–27) suggest that small firms in manufacturing and trade do reinvest a greater proportion of CBIT than large firms. In services, there again is no clear trend. In addition, small firms are likely to invest more funds in non-investment-credit property (less than 3 years of life) than large firms, judging from the fact established earlier that small firms use shorter-lived assets.

Data for 1976 on reinvestment and the other uses of CBIT are shown in table 4A–28. (The calculation of CBIT is based on net interest, not gross interest.) The table summarizes readily identifiable uses of CBIT as a fraction of CBIT—taxes and interest, dividends, and investment tax credit property. The sum of the identified uses as a fraction of CBIT is contained in the total line. A number less than one indicates additional funds were available and used internally for other uses, like working capital. A number greater than one would indicate that firms in that size category used external financing.

The data in table 4A–28 confirm those in table 4A–27 in that investment in investment tax credit property appears to be a larger fraction of CBIT for small firms. However, there is no indication in the limited data available that credit property is an alternative to dividends. For example, in manufacturing, the middle size category of firms has both low dividends and low capital investments. There appears to be more correspondence between capital investment and cash availability after taxes and interest.

The summarize, the IRS data indicate that large firms have a greater dividend payout than small firms. There is evidence that profitable small firms pay out profits in the form of excess salary, which may compensate in part for the lower dividend payout of small firms. There is also an indication that small firms reinvest a greater fraction of their cash flow than large firms, and this may account, in part, for the lower dividend payout of small firms. There does not appear to be a negative correlation between dividend payout and reinvestment, which implies that firms with sufficient cash both pay dividends and reinvest.

Dividend Regressions

This section investigates whether or not any relationship exists between dividend payout and other economic variables and firm size. Because there is not an accepted theory of an optimal dividend policy, a complete formal model is not presented and tested. Instead we focus on the relationship between dividend payout and variables reflecting firm profitability, cash availability, and firm size. We do not, for example, test the effect of double taxation of dividends or of transaction costs. Tests of the effect of dividend payment on stockholder stock market returns are conducted in chapter 6.

Previous investigators have found that the distinction between dividend-paying and non-dividend-paying companies is more critical than the distinctions among dividend-paying firms (see, for example, Miller and Scholes 1982). Consequently, two regressions are estimated—one that classifies firms into a dividend-paying and non-dividend-paying category and one that attempts to explain variations in the dividend payout among firms that pay dividends.

We first examine data for all four-digit manufacturing industries, the data for each of which is classified into 11 asset size classes. Because the smallest asset size class (0–$100,000 in assets) contains many abnormal firms (frequently in the process of going out of business), the smallest asset size category is omitted. Since there are 72 four-digit manufacturing industries and 10 size classes, a maximum of 720 observations is available. However, observations are deleted if a cell contains no data.

The following regression is estimated over all the data:

$$DUM = a_0 + a_1 \frac{CBIT}{TA} + a_2 \frac{X}{CBIT} + a_3 S + e,$$

where

DUM = 1 if the dividend payout in the industry-size cell is zero;
$CBIT$ = Cash flow before interest and taxes;
TA = total assets;
X = ($CBIT$ − corporate income tax paid - net interest paid), a measure of cash availability;
S = an integer between 1 and 10, where 1 represents the smallest asset size class and 10 represents the largest asset size class.

The following regression is estimated over all industry-size cells that have positive dividends:

$$\frac{DIV}{CBIT} = a_0 + a_1 \frac{CBIT}{TA} + a_2 \frac{X}{CBIT} + a_3 S + e,$$

where DIV = cash dividends paid.

The results for the first regression are as follows:

$$DUM = \frac{.3732}{(10.9)} - \frac{.4009}{(-2.65)} \frac{CBIT}{TA} - \frac{.0007}{(-.05)} \frac{X}{CBIT} - \frac{.0416 S}{(-11.17)},$$
$$\bar{R}^2 = .1703, \text{ Observations } = 638,$$

where numbers in parentheses are the t ratios and $\bar{R}^2$ is the adjusted coefficient of determination. The coefficients of the independent variables should be interpreted as the change in the probability of being a non-dividend-paying cell for a unit change in the independent variable. Size is clearly significant. Small firms are less likely to pay dividends. The measure of profitability, $CBIT/TA$, is significant and negative, implying that more profitable firms are more likely to be dividend paying. The cash availability measure, $X/CBIT$, is not statistically significant.

The results for the second regression, using only positive dividend cells, are as follows:

$$\frac{DIV}{CBIT} = \frac{.2236}{(4.43)} - \frac{.0307}{(-.127)} \frac{CBIT}{TA} - \frac{.1183}{(-6.48)} \frac{X}{CBIT} - \frac{.0031 S}{(-.652)},$$
$$\bar{R}^2 = .0643, \text{ Observations } = 583,$$

where numbers in parentheses are t ratios. The coefficient of the size variable is not significantly different from zero, which implies that variations in the dividend payout, assuming the payout is positive, are not associated with firm size. The only significant variable is the cash availability measure $X/CBIT$. Contrary to expectations, the sign for this variable is negative, which implies that lower dividend payouts are associated with greater cash availability. The profitability measure is not significant.

On the basis of the regression for four-digit manufacturing industries we conclude there is a positive association between dividend payout and firm size. That association appears to be due primarily to the fact that small firms are more likely to pay no dividend.

The dividend payout decision was also analyzed for four-digit wholesale and retail trade industries and for four-digit service industries. Because firms in these industries tend to be smaller than those in manufacturing, the smallest asset size was included in the regression analysis. In trade, there are a possible 330 observations—30 four-digit industries each with 11 asset size categories. Twenty-six observations are deleted because data were missing, and 2 observations were deleted because the dividend payout was extraordinarily large—a payout ratio in excess of 1. In services, there are a possible 187 observations—17 four-digit industries each with 11 asset size categories. Twenty-seven observations are deleted because of missing data.

The percentage of cells without a dividend was small—4.4 percent in services and 1.3 percent in trade. As a result, only a single regression was estimated over all the data. The results follow:

Trade:

$$\frac{DIV}{CBIT} = \frac{.2585}{(-6.0)} + \frac{.5783}{(4.14)}\frac{CBIT}{TA} + \frac{.3590}{(5.93)}\frac{X}{CBIT} + \frac{.0118S}{(5.03)},$$
$$\bar{R}^2 = .2667, \text{ Observations } = 302;$$

Services:

$$\frac{DIV}{CBIT} = \frac{.2339}{(5.49)} - \frac{.1561}{(-1.14)}\frac{CBIT}{TA} - \frac{.1144}{(-1.99)}\frac{X}{CBIT} - \frac{.0076S}{(-2.70)},$$
$$\bar{R}^2 = .0688, \text{ Observations } = 160.$$

In trade, the dividend payout is positively related to the profitability measure, $\frac{CBIT}{TA}$, and the cash availability measure, $\frac{X}{CBIT}$. The payout also increases with firm size. In services, the coefficients have the opposite sign, although only the cash availability measure and size variable are statistically significant.

It is evident from these results that we have not found a model of the dividend payout decision that is consistent across major industrial divisions. While dividend payout tends to increase with firm size in manufacturing and trade, there tends to be a negative association of payout and size in services. The signs of the profitability and cash availability measure change from industry to industry. These inconclusive results should not be too surprising for two reasons. First, the theoretical determinants of the dividend payout are not clear since firms have alternative methods for paying out earnings. Particularly in small, closely held firms the dividend decision will hinge on the circumstances of the owners, for which we have no data, as well as the circumstances of the firm. Second, the data are not ideal for studying the dividend payout decision because firms are aggregated and because we have a snapshot for only one year at a time. Dividend payout tends to be based on permanent cash flow of the firm. Data for a particular year may fail to measure the long-run value of the variable.

Summary and Conclusion

This chapter analyzed IRS data in some detail. Our principal conclusion is that the benefits of tax deductions in the form of interest expense or other forms is less to small firms than to large firms. Small firms would also benefit less than large firms from changes in the tax code that accelerate depreciation or otherwise allow increased deductions from income. This conclusion is based on several pieces of evidence:

> Statutory tax rates are lower for small firms than for large firms, which reduces the marginal tax benefit of deductions.

> Variability of income is greater for small firms than for large firms, and this reduces the probability that the small firm will have income against which to take deductions.

> The proportion of the tentative investment tax credit actually taken is lower for small firms than for large firms, which implies that small firms are less likely to have sufficient income to use the available tax credit.

> Somewhat surprising is the evidence that depreciation is a larger fraction of cash flow for small firms than for large firms. This is probably due to the shorter life of small firms' assets. It suggests that further acceleration of depreciation expense will have less benefit to small firms than to large firms.

The impact of effective tax rates and the level of depreciation expense on capital structure is not clear. Preliminary regression analyses indicate that leverage is negatively associated with the effective tax rate and positively associated with the level of depreciation expense, contrary to our expectations based on the effect of taxes. While there are plausible explanations for some of these results, the issue deserves further analysis.

In the discussion of payout policy, we find that the largest firms tend to have a greater dividend payout than the other firms. There is also evidence that small firms pay out profits in the form of excess salary rather than dividends. The relationship of dividend payout to short-run profitability and to cash availability was examined in a regression framework. However, the results were inconsistent across major industrial divisions.

Notes

1. It also does not reflect certain other statutory special deductions, the most important of which is the intercorporate dividends received deduction.

2. The *SOI* presents data for Π = net income of firms with income less deficit of firms with deficit. The value of L is then given as $L = Y - \Pi$.

3. Note that the *SOI* cannot reflect loss carry backs.

4. A clearer size pattern is found by Stekler (1963), table 18. He finds that the three to four smallest asset size categories of manufacturing firms have a lower return on assets (measured before interest but after depreciation) than middle- or large-sized firms. Further investigation of this issue appears to be warranted.

5. If $k = \dfrac{\text{loans from stockholders}}{\text{total assets}}$, the adjusted measure of leverage would be $\dfrac{1}{1 + k\dfrac{A}{S}} \cdot \dfrac{A}{S}$, where $\dfrac{A}{S}$ is $\dfrac{\text{total assets}}{\text{total equity}}$, the ratio reported in table 4A–20. The data for k are not, however, available for individual industries. Assuming $k = .08$ and $\dfrac{A}{S} = 2.8$ would imply an adjustment factor of $1/\left(1 + k\dfrac{A}{S}\right) = .82$.

6. The reliability of the data in the largest size category is suspect because few service firms are in that category.

Appendix 4A: Tables

Table 4A–1
Marginal Corporate Tax Rate, 1973–1980
(percentages)

Taxable Income ($ Thousand)	*1973–1974*	*1975–1978*	*1979–1980*
0–25	0.22	0.20	0.17
25–50	0.48	0.22	0.20
50–75	0.48	0.48	0.30
75–100	0.48	0.48	0.40
100 +	0.48	0.48	0.46

Table 4A–2
Number of Corporations with Net Income as a Fraction of All Active Corporations, by Asset Size and Year, 1973–1979

	Asset Size ($ Million)											
Year	0–0.1	0.1–0.25	0.25–0.5	0.5–1	1–5	5–10	10–25	25–50	50–100	100–250	250+
1973	.5442	.7375	.7753	.7795	.7689	.8026	.8398	.8563	.8517	.8525	.8646
1974	.5304	.7179	.7598	.7696	.7489	.7626	.7927	.8033	.8002	.7810	.7778
1975	.5256	.7061	.7518	.7683	.7577	.7671	.7749	.7819	.7714	.7823	.7822
1976	.5271	.6957	.7517	.7738	.7748	.7968	.8152	.8358	.8401	.8313	.8371
1977	.5504	.7197	.7600	.7805	.7887	.7867	.8351	.8760	.8720	.8585	.8898
1978	.5513	.7277	.7714	.7944	.7988	.8112	.8460	.8838	.8805	.8705	.9051
1979	.5326	.7018	.7541	.7573	.7816	.7721	.8187	.8559	.8512	.8496	.8612

Table 4A–3
Income of Corporations with Income as a Fraction of the Sum of (a) Income of Corporations with Income and (b) Losses of Corporations with Losses, by Asset Size, All Industries, 1973–1979

Year	Asset Size ($ Million)										
	0–0.1	0.1–0.25	0.25–0.5	0.5–1	1–5	5–10	10–25	25–50	50–100	100–250	250+
1973	.5757	.7471	.7879	.8019	.8280	.8413	.8423	.8669	.8761	.9176	.9692
1974	.5333	.7355	.7660	.8010	.8055	.8051	.8046	.8252	.8444	.8615	.9516
1975	.5286	.6963	.7602	.7911	.8038	.7969	.8165	.8361	.8327	.8407	.9456
1976	.5398	.7097	.7560	.7935	.8189	.8386	.8503	.8871	.8756	.8864	.9673
1977	.5784	.7354	.7657	.8095	.8310	.8506	.8722	.8934	.9016	.9090	.9705
1978	.5849	.7669	.7927	.8246	.8360	.8581	.8711	.9025	.9117	.9148	.9751
1979	.5631	.7276	.7785	.7567	.8199	.8297	.8530	.8549	.8951	.8962	.9692

Table 4A–4
Income of Corporations with Income as a Fraction of the Sum of Income of Corporations with Income and Losses of Corporations with Losses, for Selected Industries and Asset Sizes, 1973–1979

Industry and Asset Size ($ Million)	1973	1974	1975	1976	1977	1978	1979
Manufacturing							
0.1–0.25	.7048	.6637	.6090	.6397	.6230	.7500	.7048
5–10	.8844	.8441	.8523	.8869	.8902	.8931	.8549
250+	.9873	.9798	.9725	.9790	.9642	.9799	.9732
Trade							
0.1–0.25	.8094	.8208	.7482	.7547	.7745	.7868	.7380
5–10	.9130	.8815	.8958	.8893	.9299	.7066	.9013
250+	.9540	.8456	.8254	.9549	.9805	.9765	.9858
Service							
0.1–0.25	.6726	.7116	.7116	.7554	.7818	.7848	.7509
5–10	.7868	.6280	.6676	.7182	.7142	.8167	.7512
250+	.9392	.7986	.9248	.9729	.9868	.9854	.9526

Table 4A–5
Net Operating Loss Deduction as a Fraction of Non-1120S Corporations' Net Income, by Asset Size, 1976

Industry	All	0	0–0.1	0.1–0.25	0.25–0.50	0.50–1	1–5	5–10	10–25	25–50	50–100	100–250	250+
							Asset Size ($ Million)						
Agriculture, forestry, and fishing	.1218	.0121	.1562	.1116	.0857	.1491	.1580	.1676	.1476	.5249	.1576	—	—
Mining	.0078	.0793	.2234	.2333	.1088	.1232	.0664	.0556	.0955	.0918	.0798	.0179	.0031
Construction	.1114	.3551	.2686	.1365	.1106	.1135	.1049	.0959	.0890	.1203	.1378	.0605	.0352
Manufacturing	.0187	.0493	.3243	.1431	.0760	.0569	.0502	.0391	.0386	.0304	.0431	.0179	.0082
Transportation and public utilities	.0515	.0453	.2008	.1564	.0797	.1026	.0660	.0982	.0536	.0469	.1126	.0475	.0446
Wholesale and retail trade	.0391	.0789	.2047	.0663	.0485	.0407	.0284	.0285	.0369	.0520	.0407	.0247	.0167
Finance	.0673	.1793	.2159	.1289	.1228	.1094	.1342	.1467	.1103	.0773	.0819	.0697	.0318
Services	.1282	.3456	.1948	.1317	.1256	.1041	.1404	.0970	.1009	.0816	.0732	.0851	.1013

Table 4A–6
Alternative Tax Rate Measures, All Industries, by Year and by Certain Asset Size Categories, 1973–1979

Tax Rate Measure and Asset Size ($ Million)	1973	1974	1975	1976	1977	1978	1979
T/II							
0.1–0.25	.2931	.3011	.3051	.2669	.2510	.2336	.2331
5–10	.4793	.4974	.5026	.4713	.4583	.4580	.4476
250+	.4373	.4487	.4709	.4580	.4549	.4533	.4319
T/YT							
0.1–0.25	.2890	.2876	.2400	.2334	.2378	.2341	.1720
5–10	.4604	.4636	.4565	.4567	.4564	.4552	.4312
250+	.4753	.4770	.4763	.4762	.4763	.4745	.4544
T/Y							
0.1–0.25	.1939	.1928	.1721	.1577	.1607	.1626	.1458
5–10	.3889	.3778	.3746	.3806	.3779	.3822	.3557
250+	.4234	.4258	.4439	.4425	.4411	.4417	.4181
T/CBIT							
0.1–0.25	.1316	.1296	.1183	.1082	.1156	.1143	.1000
5–10	.2258	.2244	.2199	.2318	.2309	.2278	.2051
250+	.1784	.1873	.1914	.2127	.2130	.2000	.1849
$(T - G)/CBIT$							
0.1–0.25	.1213	.1182	.1037	.0919	.0798	.0678	.0659
5–10	.2123	.2114	.2032	.2083	.1950	.1881	.1782
250+	.1107	.0843	.0832	.0995	.1020	.1016	.0805

Table 4A–7
Alternative Tax Rate Measures, Manufacturing, by Year and by Certain Asset Size Categories, 1973–1979

Tax Rate Measure and Asset Size ($ Million)	1973	1974	1975	1976	1977	1978	1979
T/Π							
0.1–0.25	.3652	.4024	.4570	.3832	.4693	.2546	.2569
5–10	.4959	.5384	.5216	.5004	.4927	.4936	.5019
250+	.4366	.4209	.4633	.4570	.4726	.4667	.4465
T/YT							
0.1–0.25	.2913	.2837	.2299	.2314	.2455	.2359	.1981
5–10	.4678	.4709	.4661	.4662	.4660	.4629	.4416
250+	.4743	.4742	.4744	.4737	.4741	.4719	.4505
T/Y							
0.1–0.25	.2122	.1985	.1636	.1674	.1853	.1698	.1493
5–10	.4311	.4390	.4312	.4365	.4319	.4346	.4167
250+	.4310	.4123	.4502	.4472	.4550	.4571	.4342
T/CBIT							
0.1–0.25	.1608	.1487	.1340	.1339	.1608	.1323	.1116
5–10	.3070	.3071	.3094	.3173	.3129	.3062	.2783
250+	.2541	.2463	.2517	.2729	.2756	.2702	.2567
(T − G)/CBIT							
0.1–0.25	.1421	.1295	.1076	.1050	.0947	.0603	.0632
5–10	.2896	.2903	.2891	.2827	.2600	.2557	.2442
250+	.1626	.1389	.1336	.1665	.1649	.1614	.1350

Table 4A–8
Alternative Tax Rate Measures, Wholesale and Retail Trade, by Year and by Certain Asset Size Categories, 1973–1979

Tax Rate Measure and Asset Size ($ Million)	1973	1974	1975	1976	1977	1978	1979
T/II							
0.1–0.25	.2621	.2526	.2588	.2311	.2225	.2119	.2199
5–10	.3963	.3703	.3716	.3855	.3754	.3848	.3487
250+	.4747	.4826	.4967	.4066	.3797	.3694	.3399
T/YT							
0.1–0.25	.2965	.2946	.2444	.2349	.2339	.2246	.1998
5–10	.4691	.4695	.4617	.4617	.4605	.4580	.4337
250+	.4760	.4791	.4783	.4781	.4786	.4669	.4554
T/Y							
0.1–0.25	.2004	.1975	.1717	.1560	.1577	.1545	.1418
5–10	.3585	.3206	.3283	.3375	.3472	.3474	.3105
250+	.4518	.3945	.3916	.3874	.3721	.3605	.3350
T/CBIT							
0.1–0.25	.1525	.1473	.1314	.1157	.1205	.1126	.1051
5–10	.2674	.2475	.2370	.2413	.2376	.2822	.1901
250+	.2208	.1775	.2181	.2314	.2267	.2143	.1855
(*T* − *G*)/CBIT							
0.1–0.25	.1448	.1395	.1205	.1036	.0913	.0713	.0741
5–10	.2560	.2381	.2227	.2256	.2096	.2388	.1695
250+	.1740	.1210	.1765	.1466	.1600	.1578	.1241

Table 4A–9
Alternative Tax Rate Measures, Services, by Year and by Certain Asset Size Categories, 1973–1979

Tax Rate Measure and Asset Size ($ Million)	1973	1974	1975	1976	1977	1978	1979
T/II							
0.1–0.25	.3580	.3168	.3067	.2398	.2277	.2488	.2384
5–10	.5252	.8946	.7340	.6137	.5941	.4895	.5338
250+	.4206	.5889	.4645	.4307	.4634	.4633	.4664
T/YT							
0.1–0.25	.2942	.2907	.2435	.2339	.2407	.2420	.2109
5–10	.4644	.4664	.4586	.4588	.4580	.4573	.4264
250+	.4756	.4766	.4648	.4785	.3427	.4710	.4563
T/Y							
0.1–0.25	.1838	.1884	.1824	.1621	.1642	.1806	.1593
5–10	.3829	.3647	.3685	.3729	.3563	.3797	.3570
250+	.3934	.4403	.4267	.4187	.4572	.4564	.4432
T/CBIT							
0.1–0.25	.1126	.1096	.1113	.0945	.1061	.1173	.0975
5–10	.1327	.1264	.1420	.1549	.1470	.1527	.1421
250+	.1011	.0844	.0980	.1057	.1332	.1234	.1336
(T − G)/CBIT							
0.1–0.25	.1001	.0951	.0919	.0742	.0612	.0658	.0585
5–10	.1145	.1149	.1248	.1299	.1209	.1166	.1168
250+	.0667	.0433	.0589	.0666	.0826	.0848	.0941

Table 4A–10
Tax Liability as a Fraction of Alternative Measures of Income Excluding Income of 1120S Corporations, by Selected Industries and Asset Sizes, 1976

	Asset Size ($ Million)		
Ratio and Industry	0.1–0.25	5–10	250+
T/Y'			
All Industries	.2049	.4195	.4500
Manufacturing	.1975	.4441	.4469
Trade	.2183	.4437	.4642
Services	.2011	.4054	.4152
T/II'			
All industries	.3332	.4821	.4579
Manufacturing	.4378	.5093	.4569
Trade	.2929	.3927	.4066
Services	.2927	.6464	.4307

Table 4A–11
Marginal Effective Expected Tax Rate, by Certain Size Categories and Certain Industries, 1973–1979

Industry and Asset Size ($ Million)	1973	1974	1975	1976	1977	1978	1979
All industries							
0.1–0.25	.2159	.2115	.1671	.1656	.1749	.1795	.1251
5–10	.3873	.3737	.3638	.3830	.3882	.3906	.3578
250+	.4607	.4539	.4504	.4606	.4622	.4627	.4404
Manufacturing							
0.1–0.25	.2053	.1883	.1400	.1480	.1529	.1769	.1396
5–10	.4137	.3975	.3973	.4135	.4148	.4134	.3775
250+	.4683	.4646	.4614	.4638	.4571	.4624	.4384
Trade							
0.1–0.25	.2400	.2418	.1829	.1773	.1812	.1767	.1475
5–10	.4283	.4139	.4136	.4106	.4282	.3236	.3909
250+	.4541	.4051	.3948	.4565	.4693	.4559	.4489
Services							
0.1–0.25	.1979	.2069	.1733	.1767	.1882	.1899	.1584
5–10	.3654	.2929	.3062	.3295	.3271	.3735	.3203
250+	.4467	.3806	.4298	.4655	.3382	.4641	.4347

Table 4A–12
Investment Tax Credit as a Fraction of the Cost of Property Used for Investment Credit, by Selected Industries and Asset Sizes, 1974–1979

Industry and Asset Size ($ Million)	1974	1975	1976	1977	1978	1979
All industries						
0.1–0.25	.0311	.0362	.0375	.0381	.0408	.0401
5–10	.0418	.0519	.0565	.0552	.0594	.0576
250+	.0433	.0601	.0722	.0725	.0739	.0695
Manufacturing						
0.1–0.25	.0347	.0452	.0485	.0449	.0473	.0496
5–10	.0515	.0680	.0700	.0735	.0780	.0706
250+	.0589	.0592	.0702	.0688	.0766	.0938
Trade						
0.1–0.25	.0279	.0331	.0328	.0386	.0402	.0402
5–10	.0438	.0460	.0533	.0556	.0555	.0548
250+	.0578	.0764	.0770	.0818	.0867	.0821
Services						
0.1–0.25	.0342	.0382	.0399	.0411	.0408	.0403
5–10	.0209	.0258	.0348	.0246	.0313	.0343
250+	.0347	.0623	.0534	.0720	.0574	.0548

Table 4A–13

Total Qualified Investment as a Fraction of the Total Cost of Investment Tax Credit Property (P_2/P_1) and Investment Tax Credit as a Fraction of Total Tentative Credit (ITC/TTC), by Selected Industries and Asset Sizes, 1976

	Asset Size ($ Million)		
Ratio and Industry	*0.1–0.25*	*5–10*	*250+*
P_2/P_1			
All Industries	.5978	.7965	.7927
Manufacturing	.7071	.8512	.7811
Trade	.5282	.7465	.9362
Service	.6547	.6732	.7339
ITC/TTC			
All industries	.4883	.5050	.6562
Manufacturing	.5039	.6115	.7449
Trade	.4976	.5645	.6920
Service	.4907	.3301	.3750

Table 4A–14

Foreign Tax Credit as a Fraction of CBIT, by Industry and Asset Size, 1973–1979

Industry and Asset Size ($ Million)	*1973*	*1974*	*1975*	*1976*	*1977*	*1978*	*1979*
All industries							
0.1–0.25	.0001	.0000	.0000	.0001	.0003	.0002	.0000
5–10	.0021	.0022	.0024	.0021	.0021	.0031	.0017
250+	.0533	.0905	.0876	.0868	.0831	.0717	.0798
Manufacturing							
0.1–0.25	.0000	.0000	.0001	.0002	.0001	.0000	.0000
5–10	.0026	.0022	.0024	.0023	.0032	.0038	.0033
250+	.0742	.0903	.0941	.0750	.0802	.0805	.0867
Trade							
0.1–0.25	.0000	.0000	.0000	.0002	.0001	.0000	.0000
5–10	.0023	.0011	.0022	.0023	.0008	.0037	.0003
250+	.0339	.0417	.0190	.0657	.0471	.0348	.0389
Services							
0.1–0.25	.0000	.0000	.0000	.0000	.0002	.0008	.0000
5–10	.0021	.0011	.0022	.0056	.0029	.0075	.0036
250+	.0139	.0202	.0123	.0153	.0147	.0116	.0117

Table 4A–15
CBIT as a Fraction of Total Receipts, by Selected Industries and Asset Sizes, 1973–1979

Industry and Asset Size ($ Million)	1973	1974	1975	1976	1977	1978	1979
All industries							
0.1–0.25	.0560	.0556	.0541	.0537	.0584	.0602	.0561
5–10	.0831	.0829	.0809	.0758	.0754	.0734	.0725
250 +	.1602	.1562	.1527	.1561	.1568	.1607	.1638
Manufacturing							
0.1–0.25	.0504	.0525	.0463	.0489	.0492	.0629	.0594
5–10	.0808	.0769	.0774	.0784	.0814	.0826	.0777
250 +	.1208	.1069	.1060	.1122	.1129	.1158	.1165
Trade							
0.1–0.25	.0387	.0396	.0360	.0353	.0396	.0400	.0385
5–10	.0461	.0519	.0487	.0433	.0442	.0353	.0457
250 +	.0513	.0430	.0436	.0468	.0474	.0502	.0507
Services							
0.1–0.25	.0743	.0766	.0763	.0765	.0747	.0764	.0676
5–10	.1764	.1589	.1607	.1513	.1380	.1469	.1348
250 +	.1838	.2022	.2394	.2422	.2530	.2535	.2313

Table 4A–16
CBIT as a Fraction of Total Assets, by Selected Industries and Asset Sizes, 1973–1979

Industry and Asset Size ($ Million)	1973	1974	1975	1976	1977	1978	1979
All industries							
0.1–0.25	.1213	.1238	.1195	.1222	.1346	.1480	.1430
5–10	.0910	.0974	.1003	.1046	.1087	.1200	.1232
250 +	.0743	.0862	.0794	.0844	.0852	.0871	.0947
Manufacturing							
0.1–0.25	.1260	.1302	.1142	.1270	.1292	.1716	.1613
5–10	.1487	.1492	.1467	.1588	.1600	.1700	.1628
250 +	.1351	.1404	.1277	.1404	.1385	.1421	.1455
Trade							
0.1–0.25	.1259	.1306	.1174	.1188	.1289	.1359	.1372
5–10	.1338	.1506	.1397	.1307	.1356	.1082	.1433
250 +	.0978	.0944	.1001	.1064	.1166	.1228	.1247
Service							
0.1–0.25	.1401	.1532	.1544	.1614	.1712	.1896	.1809
5–10	.1577	.1291	.1435	.1439	.1226	.1741	.1688
250 +	.1102	.1350	.1632	.1650	.1777	.1704	.1587

Table 4A–17
Depreciation Expense as a Fraction of CBIT, by Certain Asset Size Categories and Certain Industries, 1973–1979

Industry and Asset Size ($ Million)	1973	1974	1975	1976	1977	1978	1979
All industries							
0.1–0.25	.3630	.3664	.3927	.3847	.3514	.3287	.3612
5–10	.2412	.2348	.2478	.2472	.2527	.2510	.2537
250+	.2382	.2073	.2335	.2162	.2152	.2102	.1889
Manufacturing							
0.1–0.25	.4034	.4405	.4953	.4512	.4563	.3244	.3857
5–10	.2347	.2458	.2421	.2315	.2377	.2277	.2465
250+	.2612	.2457	.2775	.2529	.2659	.2595	.2459
Trade							
0.1–0.25	.2695	.2593	.2992	.3073	.2793	.2892	.3046
5–10	.1565	.1531	.1801	.1960	.1924	.2491	.1914
250+	.2144	.2114	.2340	.2046	.1984	.1891	.1823
Services							
0.1–0.25	.5114	.4760	.4636	.4436	.3919	.3858	.4219
5–10	.5333	.5440	.5206	.4781	.4925	.4706	.4595
250+	.5076	.5596	.5611	.5450	.5255	.5236	.4679

Table 4A–18
Gross Interest Expense as a Fraction of CBIT, by Certain Asset Size Categories and Certain Industries, 1973–1979

Industry and Asset Size ($ Million)	1973	1974	1975	1976	1977	1978	1979
All industries							
0.1–0.25	.1879	.2032	.2197	.2100	.1881	.1819	.2098
5–10	.2876	.3140	.3147	.2609	.2436	.2516	.2880
250+	.3537	.3752	.3601	.3193	.3166	.3486	.3831
Manufacturing							
0.1–0.25	.1563	.1898	.2115	.1995	.2010	.1561	.1797
5–10	.1462	.1839	.1647	.1344	.1273	.1521	.1990
250+	.1568	.1692	.1793	.1499	.1508	.1615	.1793
Trade							
0.1–0.25	.1487	.1576	.1932	.1922 ·	.1789	.1793	.2175
5–10	.1688	.1786	.1821	.1781	.1748	.2760	.2634
250+	.3203	.4207	.3269	.2263	.2045	.2307	.2718
Service							
0.1–0.25	.1741	.1781	.1737	.1625	.1422	.1428	.1689
5–10	.2140	.3147	.2859	.2687	.2601	.2174	.2743
250+	.2520	.2971	.2279	.2096	.1870	.2100	.2456

Table 4A–19
Net Interest Paid as a Fraction of CBIT, by Certain Asset Size Categories and
Certain Industries, All Firms and Firms with Income, 1976

Industrial Division and Interest Variable	Asset Size Category ($ Million)		
	1–25	*5–10*	*250+*
All industries			
Net interest, all firms	.1617	.0606	−.1288
Net interest, income firms	.0759	.0106	−.1035
Manufacturing			
Net interest, all firms	.1653	.1052	.0746
Net interest, income firms	.0652	.0693	.0635
Wholesale and retail trade			
Net interest, all firms	.1610	.1118	.1040
Net interest, income firms	.0827	.0690	.0864
Services			
Net interest, all firms	.1235	.2260	.1219
Net interest, income firms	.0698	.1469	.1138

CBIT = Π + N + I, where N = depreciation and other noncash charges and I = interest expenses net of interest revenues.

Table 4A–20
Ratio of Total Assets to Total Equity for Certain Industries and Asset Sizes,
1973–1979

Industry and Asset Size ($ Million)	1973	1974	1975	1976	1977	1978	1979
All industries							
0.1–0.25	2.64	2.65	2.66	2.73	2.81	2.86	2.98
5–10	3.63	3.63	3.55	3.30	3.27	3.31	3.28
250+	3.87	4.08	4.02	4.03	4.05	4.16	4.10
Manufacturing							
0.1–0.25	2.56	2.81	2.68	2.78	3.04	2.99	3.49
5–10	2.08	2.11	2.19	2.06	2.04	2.17	2.24
250+	2.06	2.16	2.15	2.20	2.18	2.21	2.27
Trade							
0.1–0.25	2.43	2.43	2.52	2.65	2.70	2.79	2.99
5–10	2.72	2.69	2.52	2.64	2.75	2.98	2.89
250+	2.62	2.71	2.88	2.69	2.58	2.69	2.98
Services							
0.1–0.25	2.86	2.78	2.76	2.85	2.80	2.80	2.82
5–10	3.17	4.11	5.30	4.40	4.13	3.95	4.29
250+	2.58	2.92	2.90	3.04	2.98	3.06	2.95

Table 4A–21
Ratio of Total Assets Less Current Liabilities to Total Equity for Certain Industries and Asset Sizes, 1973–1979

Industry and Asset Size ($ Million)	1973	1974	1975	1976	1977	1978	1979
All industries							
0.1–0.25	1.76	1.77	1.78	1.83	1.85	1.91	1.97
5–10	1.74	1.77	1.77	1.70	1.72	1.72	2.32
250+	2.07	2.11	2.11	2.07	2.02	2.03	2.01
Manufacturing							
0.1–0.25	1.58	1.72	1.66	1.70	1.85	1.79	2.04
5–10	1.38	1.37	1.39	1.34	1.34	1.37	1.40
250+	1.53	1.55	1.57	1.58	1.56	1.56	1.57
Trade							
0.1–0.25	1.51	1.54	1.59	1.66	1.71	1.76	1.85
5–10	1.38	1.41	1.38	1.38	1.41	1.49	1.45
250+	1.51	1.54	1.62	1.56	1.50	1.57	1.75
Services							
0.1–0.25	2.01	1.91	1.92	1.97	1.94	1.99	1.99
5–10	2.26	2.98	3.51	2.95	2.75	2.53	2.75
250+	1.92	2.00	2.00	1.98	1.91	2.02	1.81

Table 4A–22
Loans to Stockholders and Loans from Stockholders as a Fraction of Total Assets, All Industries, 1973–1979

Ratio and Asset Size ($ Million)	1973	1974	1975	1976	1977	1978	1979
Loans to stockholders							
0–0.1	.030	.032	.033	.035	.037	.039	.043
0.1–0.25	.017	.018	.020	.021	.023	.026	.031
0.25–0.50	.011	.012	.011	.012	.013	.015	.020
0.5–1	.008	.008	.009	.010	.011	.012	.014
1–5	.005	.006	.006	.007	.007	.007	.008
Loans from stockholders							
0–0.1	.132	.146	.160	.174	.179	.175	.184
0.1–0.25	.069	.076	.077	.087	.090	.092	.097
0.25–0.5	.046	.050	.056	.055	.058	.065	.072
0.5–1	.036	.038	.042	.043	.042	.047	.050
1–5	.021	.021	.022	.023	.024	.025	.029

Table 4A–23
Ratio of Current Liabilities to Long-Term Debt for Certain Industries and Asset Sizes, 1973–1979

Industry and Asset Size ($ Million)	1973	1974	1975	1976	1977	1978	1979
All industries							
0.1–0.25	1.79	1.76	1.76	1.73	1.81	1.66	1.73
5–10	3.58	3.32	3.17	3.05	2.86	2.93	1.77
250+	3.47	3.63	3.46	3.57	3.90	4.02	4.05
Manufacturing							
0.1–0.25	2.65	2.50	2.38	2.41	2.32	2.69	2.30
5–10	2.38	2.56	2.80	2.60	2.63	2.60	2.57
250+	1.43	1.61	1.40	1.43	1.55	1.56	1.75
Trade							
0.1–0.25	3.06	2.83	2.66	2.47	2.43	2.16	2.23
5–10	4.52	4.27	3.88	4.41	4.28	3.76	4.06
250+	2.79	2.81	2.80	2.62	2.97	2.32	2.12
Services							
0.1–0.25	1.27	1.45	1.36	1.44	1.47	1.28	1.30
5–10	.91	.70	.90	.92	.96	1.16	1.06
250+	.91	1.12	1.14	1.27	1.45	1.34	1.73

Table 4A–24
Leverage Regression Results for Four-Digit Industries, 1976

$$\frac{B^1}{TA} = a_0 + a_1 t^* + a_2 \frac{N}{TA} + a_3 S$$

Industry	a_0	a_1	a_2	a_3	$\bar{R}^2$	S.E.	Obs.
Manufacturing	.2046 (12.36)	−.3995 (−8.36)	.9009 (5.80)	.0173 (9.45)	.181	.085	628
Trade	.0588 (3.87)	−.2302 (−5.63)	2.710 (9.15)	.0175 (11.41)	.389	.042	272
Services	.3479 (8.90)	−.6359 (−4.75)	.6781 (3.16)	.0268 (4.724)	.194	.134	144

Source: IRS *Source Book,* 1976.

Notes: Numbers in parentheses are *t* ratios. S.E. = standard error of the residuals. Obs. = number of observations = (10 size classes) (number of four-digit industries).

Table 4A–25
Cash Dividends as a Fraction of CBIT for Certain Industries and Asset Sizes, 1973–1979

Industry and Asset Size ($ Million)	1973	1974	1975	1976	1977	1978	1979
All industries							
0.1–0.25	.0976	.0866	.0852	.0945	.0979	.0679	.0674
5–10	.0688	.0779	.0830	.0840	.0849	.0719	.0752
250+	.1816	.1639	.1440	.1518	.1445	.1451	.1439
Manufacturing							
0.1–0.25	.0618	.0565	.0790	.0878	.0559	.0458	.0475
5–10	.0643	.0671	.0644	.0684	.0683	.0534	.0550
250+	.1924	.1730	.1908	.1805	.1855	.1885	.1904
Trade							
0.1–0.25	.1085	.0849	.0776	.1052	.0985	.0778	.0726
5–10	.0708	.0985	.1124	.1083	.1188	.1244	.1030
250+	.1384	.1322	.1570	.1249	.1693	.1563	.1443
Services							
0.1–0.25	.0934	.0944	.0498	.0594	.1031	.0440	.0411
5–10	.0356	.0479	.0460	.0584	.0568	.0501	.0547
250+	.1041	.0485	.0374	.0447	.0394	.0563	.0676

Table 4A–26
Dividend Payout, Employee Benefits as a Fraction of Total Receipts, and Excess Officer Compensation of Profitable Firms as a Fraction of CBIT, by Certain Industries and Asset Sizes, 1976

Industry and Ratio	Asset Size ($ Million)		
	0.1–0.25	*5–10*	*250+*
All industries			
Dividend/*CBIT*	.0995	.1047	.2453
Benefits/Total receipts	.0076	.0081	.0191
EC/CBIT	.1764	.0198	− .0306
Manufacturing			
Dividend/*CBIT*	.0909	.0699	.1889
Benefits/Total receipts	.0086	.0110	.0226
EC/CBIT	.2334	.0190	− .0043
Trade			
Dividend/*CBIT*	.1088	.1168	.1441
Benefits/Total receipts	.0038	.0043	.0064
EC/CBIT	.1828	.0369	.0019
Services			
Dividend/*CBIT*	.0619	.0613	.0494[a]
Benefits/Total receipts	.0212	.0130	.0113
EC/CBIT	.3379	.0002	.0002

[a]There are relatively few observations in this size category, and the ratio appears abnormal. The next two smaller size classes have ratios of .0914 and .1042 respectively.

Table 4A–27
Cost of Investment Tax Credit Property as a Fraction of CBIT, by Certain Industries and Certain Asset Sizes, 1974–1979

Industry and Asset Size ($ Million)	*1974*	*1975*	*1976*	*1977*	*1978*	*1979*
All industries						
0.1–0.25	.3633	.4010	.4265	.4454	.4542	.4868
5–10	.2602	.2769	.2961	.3264	.3268	.3410
250+	.2869	.3423	.3608	.3722	.3552	.3435
Manufacturing						
0.1–0.25	.5533	.5791	.5742	.7278	.5723	.6081
5–10	.2815	.2637	.2852	.3170	.3138	.3320
250+	.2893	.4036	.4357	.4218	.3612	.3587
Trade						
0.1–0.25	.2803	.3278	.3584	.3446	.3879	.3695
5–10	.1901	.2635	.2506	.2575	.3359	.2821
250+	.2568	.2943	.2478	.2349	.2444	.2621
Services						
0.1–0.25	.4214	.5063	.5069	.4720	.5171	.5775
5–10	.5004	.5827	.5464	.6130	.5242	.4973
250+	.6011	.4311	.4436	.4589	.4600	.5007

Table 4A–28
Uses of CBIT as a Fraction of CBIT, 1976

Industry and Ratio	Asset Size ($ Million)		
	0.1–0.25	5–10	250+
All industries[a]			
Taxes and interest	.2587	.3259	.0327
Dividends	.0995	.1047	.2453
Investment tax credit property	.4493	.3690	.5830
Total	.8075	.7995	.8610
Manufacturing			
Taxes and interest	.2749	.4066	.2498
Dividends	.0909	.0699	.1889
Investment tax credit property	.5945	.2913	.4560
Total	.9604	.7677	.8946
Trade			
Taxes and interest	.2682	.3550	.2731
Dividends	.1088	.1168	.1441
Investment tax credit property	.3706	.2702	.2859
Total	.7476	.7420	.7031
Services			
Taxes and interest	.2008	.3628	.1956[b]
Dividends	.0619	.0613	.0494
Investment tax·credit property	.5285	.5736	.4908
Total	.7913	.9977	.7359

[a]All industries' data are confounded by inclusion of financial corporations that have negative net interest expense that reduces what is paid out in interest for all corporations.

[b]As noted before, the data in the largest size category in services are suspect because there are relatively few firms. The corresponding numbers for the next smaller size category are .3300, .0914, .5228, .9441.

5
An Empirical Examination of the Relationship between Firm Size and Corporate Leverage

Modigliani and Miller (1958) showed that the value of the firm is not affected by its capital structure when markets are frictionless and there are no corporate taxes. The inclusion of corporate taxes in the Modigliani-Miller model suggests that the addition of debt to the firm's capital structure increases the value of the firm by the present value of the tax savings provided by the deduction for interest expense. This implies that the total value of the firm is maximized when the firm's assets are financed entirely by the issuance of debt. DeAngelo and Masulis (1980) have shown that the variability of the firm's cash flow from operations and the existence of nondebt tax shields in the form of depreciation expense and investment tax credits limit the ability of the firm to use the tax deduction fully for interest expense in any given year. Although the corporate tax code provides for the carry forward of a net operating loss (that is, the carry forward of unused tax deductions to offset income in future periods), the delay in the use of the tax deduction for interest expense is costly to the firm. Consequently, uncertainty about the future level of income from operations and the existence of substitutes for the tax deduction for interest expense may cause the firm to maximize value by choosing a capital structure having both debt and equity. This is usually referred to as the firm's *optimal capital structure.*

The work of DeAngelo and Masulis (1980) suggests that the amount of debt in a firm's capital structure should be negatively related to both the variability of the firm's operating income and the firm's tax deductions for depreciation expense, which serve as a substitute for the tax deductions for interest expense. The model of capital structure developed in chapter 3 extends the work of DeAngelo and Masulis by showing that the variability of operating income may be related to firm size. The model shows that if the operating cash flows of the divisions of a large firm are less than perfectly correlated, then the relative variability (in relation to total assets) of a large firm will be less than that of a smaller firm. This was shown to imply that a firm's optimal debt to total assets ratio is positively related to firm size. In addition, the model implies that a firm's debt to total assets ratio is negatively related to the coupon rate on the firm's debt.

The predictions of the model are tested empirically in this chapter. In addition to the explicit predictions of the theoretical model, the empirical model will also consider the effects of industry classification and dividend policy on the firm's leverage decision. The research methodology and the predictions of the model are discussed first. This is followed by a description of the data and presentation of the empirical results. An alternative specification of the empirical model is considered next, followed by conclusions.

Research Methodology

The theory of capital structure that has been elaborated by DeAngelo and Masulis (1980) predicts that a firm has a unique optimal capital structure. This prediction is the result of the fact that firms have tax shields in the form of depreciation expense and investment tax credits that serve as a substitute for the tax deduction for interest expense. Since the ability of the firm to use tax deductions is limited by net cash flow from operations, firms with large amounts of tax shield substitutes should limit the amount of debt in their capital structure to avoid the loss that occurs when the firm fails to use all its tax shields in a given year. Although a net operating loss may be carried forward to offset future income, the failure to realize the tax benefits of a deduction in the current period is costly to the firm.

These results were extended in chapter 3, where the firm's debt to total assets ratio was shown to be positively related to firm size. The model emphasizes the fact that the probability that a firm will be able to use a given amount of tax deductions in any given year is determined by the variability of its cash flow from operations. The more variable the firm's operating cash flow, the greater is the probability that the firm will fail to use all its available tax shields fully. Consequently, the amount of debt in a firm's capital structure may be limited by the variability of its revenue stream. The model shows that a firm's variability of cash flow per unit of assets (relative variability) is related to firm size. This relation results from the fact that the cash flows of the components of a large firm will tend to be less than perfectly correlated, creating a diversification effect that causes the relative variability of a large firm's cash flow to be less than the average of the relative variabilities of the cash flows of its components. This implies that, holding the probability of fully using available tax shields constant, large firms will choose a greater debt to total assets ratio than will small firms.

This line of reasoning was shown to imply that the ratio of the book value of debt to the book value of total assets can be expressed as

$$\frac{D}{K} = \frac{1}{r} \left\{ (\bar{\theta} - \alpha) - t\sigma \left[\rho + \frac{1}{N}(1 - \rho) \right]^{1/2} \right\},$$

where

D = the book value of the firm's debt;

K = the book value of total assets;

r = the coupon rate on the firm's debt;

$\bar{\theta}$ = the mean productivity per unit of capital;

σ = the variance of the productivity of capital;

ρ = the correlation between the output of the divisions of a large firm, $0 < \rho < 1$;

α = the rate at which capital depreciates;

N = the size of the firm in standardized units;

t = the level of confidence that the firm will fully utilize all tax shields.

The model predicts that a firm's debt to total assets ratio is positively related to firm size and the mean productivity of capital and is negatively related to the coupon rate on debt, the rate at which capital depreciates, and the variability of cash flow from operations.

We tested these predictions using a cross-sectional regression of alternative measures of the debt to total assets ratio on a set of proxies for the determinants of capital structure suggested by the model. Since the model makes no distinction between current liabilities and long-term debt, four different versions of the dependent variable are employed in the empirical tests of the model. The first, *DTA1*, is the ratio of long-term debt to total assets. The debt to total assets ratio is also measured by the ratio of long-term debt plus current liabilities to total assets, *DTA2*. The rationale behind the use of this measure of leverage is the fact that stretching accounts payable and short-term financing is to some degree a substitute for long-term debt. Although accounts payable often have no explicit cost to the firm in terms of interest expense, their presence on the balance sheet may, at the margin, limit the ability of the firm to issue long-term debt.

Cash and short-term investments can be used either to reduce the firm's current liabilities or to retire long-term debt. In addition, short-term investments generate interest income, and this income offsets the tax deduction provided by interest expense. This concept implies that cash and short-term investments can be thought of as an offset to the firm's debt. The final two measures of the debt to total assets ratio that are considered are modifications of *DTA1* and *DAT2* to reflect the cash and short-term investment position of the firm. *DTA3* uses long-term debt less cash and short-term investments as the measure of debt in the debt to total assets ratio while *DTA4* uses long-term debt plus current liabilities less cash and short-term investments.

Note that the book values of debt and total assets have been used to measure the debt to total assets ratio. The use of book values rather than market values is appropriate only in a single-period model or in a world where the cost of borrowing is nonstochastic. Since neither situation accurately describes the environment from which the data are taken, the debt to total assets ratio should be estimated using market values. Book values have been used since neither the market values of long-term debt or total assets were readily available. This creates an errors-in-variables problem. However, the coefficients of the independent variables in an ordinary least squares regression will be unbiased as long as the observation errors are uncorrelated with the independent variables. In any event, the error of approximation is likely to be small since changes in the market value of the firm's debt should be highly correlated with changes in the market value of assets.

The proxies for the determinants of capital structure have been calculated using data that were available prior to the observation of the debt to total assets ratio. For example, the cross-sectional variation in the debt to total assets ratio calculated using balance sheet data from 1976 is regressed on independent variables that were calculated using accounting and financial data from the 6 years prior to 1976 (that is, 1970 through 1975). The procedure is repeated for each of the years 1976 through 1980. This methodology is consistent with a scenario in which a financial manager adjusts the firm's debt to total assets ratio each year using updated estimates for the parameters of a decision model that is used to determine the firm's optimal capital structure.

The model predicts that leverage is negatively related to the variability (in relation to firm size) of cash flow from operations, which in turn is negatively related to firm size. The variability of cash flow from operations has been estimated by computing an unbiased estimate of the standard deviation of net operating income plus depreciation using 6 years of data. This variability measure was then scaled by the average of net operating income plus depreciation during the 6-year sample period. In effect, the proxy for operating risk is the coefficient of variation for net operating income plus depreciation.

The effect of firm size on leverage results from the effect of firm size on the variability of operating income. In the empirical model, this effect is represented by the log of total assets for the preceding year. The firm size variable has been introduced in log form because the model predicts that relative variability is a concave function of firm size.

The two most important tax shield substitutes for the interest expense deduction are the investment tax credit and depreciation expense. A proxy for the effect of the investment tax credit has not been included in the empirical model due to the fact that the investment tax credit was not reported by a substantial number of firms in the sample. The rate at which a firm's capital depreciates was approximated by the average ratio of depreciation expense to net plant and equipment during the 3 years prior to the observation of the debt to total assets ratio.

The coupon rate on the firm's debt was estimated by computing the 3-year average ratio of interest expense to the book value of long-term debt in the preceding year. Total interest expense was used to compute this variable due to the fact that interest expense on long-term debt was available for less than 20 percent of the firms included in the sample.

In addition to the variables specified by the theoretical model, three industry dummy variables have been included in the empirical model. These variables identify firms in manufacturing, transportation, and wholesale-retail. The industry dummy variables have been included to capture the effects of factors related to membership in a particular industry that have been omitted from the model.

Empirical Results

The model was tested using data obtained from the COMPUSTAT Industrial and OTC files. The COMPUSTAT Industrial file contains financial and accounting data on approximately 2,700 companies, including all industrial companies whose common stock is listed on either the NYSE or AMEX. The OTC file contains data on approximately 850 companies that are traded over the counter. The companies included in the OTC file have been selected by Standard and Poors on the basis of investor interest as measured by the number of institutional holders, volume traded, price movement, earnings growth, and regional or economic importance. The firms included in this database are not small in the sense that an entrepreneurial venture at the local level is small. However, the COMPUSTAT database is currently the most comprehensive available source of individual firm data that can be used to examine the cross-sectional relation between firm size and capital structure.

Table 5–1 contains empirical results for the case in which the proxy for the firm's debt to total assets ratio is the ratio of the book value of long-term debt to the book value of total assets. In tables 5–2 and 5–3, the proxies for the firm's use of debt financing are, respectively, the book value of long-term debt plus current liabilities and the book value of long-term debt less cash and short-term investments. The regression results obtained using long-term debt plus current liabilities less cash and short-term investments have not been presented because the results are very similar to those presented in table 5–2.

The results presented in table 5–1 show that the debt to total assets ratio is negatively related to depreciation expense and the coupon rate on debt, as predicted by the theoretical model. This is also consistent with the DeAngelo-Masulis (1980) framework. However, the estimated coefficients of firm size and variability are not consistent with the predictions of the model. The coefficient of firm size is negative in four of the five sample periods, although the estimate is significant in only one of these periods. The coefficient of the variability measure is not significant, having a positive coefficient in three sample periods.

The results confirm the importance of industry classification in explaining capital structure. The coefficient of the dummy variable for manufacturing firms

Table 5–1
Cross-Sectional Analysis of Capital Structure

Year	Constant	Log Size	Variability	Depreciation Expense	Coupon Rate	Dummy 1	Dummy 2	Dummy 3	N	F Ratio	R^2
1976	0.308 (19.09)	-0.001 (-0.407)	0.002 (3.431)	-0.243 (-4.87)	-0.030 (-5.66)	-0.069 (-6.441)	0.035 (1.973)	-0.057 (-3.34)	1,527	23.5	.094
1977	0.354 (18.356)	-0.004 (-1.767)	0.001 (1.426)	-0.290 (-5.503)	-0.012 (-2.857)	-0.095 (-7.393)	0.046 (2.099)	-0.049 (-2.50)	1,626	22.08	.083
1978	0.315 (21.112)	-0.004 (-2.007)	-0.0001 (-1.122)	-0.173 (-4.74)	-0.009 (-3.82)	-0.074 (-7.23)	0.089 (5.155)	-0.038 (-2.755)	1,840	30.12	.099
1979	.307 (21.17)	-0.003 (-1.707)	0.0001 (0.061)	-0.170 (-4.75)	-0.008 (-3.52)	-0.067 (-6.69)	0.078 (4.57)	-0.034 (-2.465)	1,955	24.87	.079
1980	.286 (21.45)	0.002 (1.32)	-0.0001 (0.30)	-0.149 (-4.16)	-0.005 (-2.51)	-0.088 (-10.02)	0.053 (3.46)	-0.041 (-3.30)	2,018	33.06	.100

Notes: Dependent variable is $\dfrac{\text{Book value of long-term debt}}{\text{Total assets}}$. *t* statistics are in parentheses.

Table 5–2
Cross-Sectional Analysis of Capital Structure with Current Liabilities Included as Debt

Year	Constant	Log Size	Variability	Depreciation Expense	Coupon Rate	Dummy 1	Dummy 2	Dummy 3	N	F Ratio	R^2
1976	0.508 (26.11)	−0.004 (−1.73)	0.002 (2.752)	−0.065 (1.09)	−0.014 (−2.23)	−0.035 (−2.751)	0.027 (1.254)	−0.007 (−0.315)	1,527	5.70	.021
1977	0.56 (25.23)	−0.007 (−2.53)	0.001 (2.09)	−0.044 (−0.713)	−0.003 (0.55)	−0.053 (−3.57)	0.032 (1.28)	0.01 (0.49)	1,626	6.83	.025
1978	0.545 (30.79)	−0.007 (−2.74)	−0.0003 (−1.03)	−0.016 (−0.36)	0.003 (0.89)	−0.031 (−2.57)	0.067 (3.27)	0.017 (1.01)	1,840	7.59	.025
1979	0.535 (30.21)	−0.006 (−2.63)	−0.002 (0.38)	−0.016 (−0.37)	0.002 (0.76)	−0.028 (−2.31)	0.088 (4.27)	0.025 (1.50)	1,955	8.81	.027
1980	0.521 (28.31)	−0.003 (−1.07)	0.002 (4.78)	0.030 (0.60)	0.004 (1.76)	−0.054 (−4.48)	0.072 (3.41)	0.008 (0.457)	2,018	14.01	.043

Notes: Dependent variable is $\dfrac{\text{Book value of long-term debt} + \text{Current liabilities}}{\text{Total assets}}$. *t* statistics are in parentheses.

Table 5–3
Cross-Sectional Analysis of Capital Structure with Debt Reduced by Cash and Marketable Securities

Year	Constant	Log Size	Variability	Depreciation Expense	Coupon Rate	Dummy 1	Dummy 2	Dummy 3	N	F Ratio	R^2
1976	0.240 (11.57)	-0.001 (-0.299)	0.002 (2.635)	-0.387 (-6.03)	-0.037 (-5.34)	-0.061 (-4.38)	0.037 (1.60)	-0.039 (-1.75)	1,527	18.38	.074
1977	0.285 (12.56)	-0.004 (-1.36)	0.001 (1.40)	-0.399 (-6.41)	-0.013 (-2.55)	-0.088 (-5.81)	0.049 (1.90)	-0.037 (-1.57)	1,626	18.21	.069
1978	0.240 (13.42)	-0.002 (-0.94)	-0.0003 (-0.975)	-0.271 (-6.20)	-0.010	-0.061 (-4.96)	0.106 (5.13)	-0.026 (-1.57)	1,840	24.26	.081
1979	0.199 (11.12)	-0.002 (-0.83)	0.001 (0.328)	-0.246 (-5.85)	-0.008 (-3.07)	-0.045 (-3.62)	0.102 (4.87)	-0.007 (-.039)	1,955	18.76	.060
1980	0.178 (10.41)	0.010 (4.52)	-0.0001 (-0.128)	-0.238 (-5.18)	-0.006 (-2.43)	-0.084 (-7.43)	0.074 (3.79)	-0.026 (-1.66)	2,018	29.67	.090

Notes: Dependent variable is $\dfrac{\text{Book value of long-term debt} - \text{Cash and marketable securities}}{\text{Total assets}}$. t statistics are in parentheses.

(Dummy 1) is significant and negative in all five sample periods, indicating that manufacturing firms tend on average to use relatively less debt in their capital structures. This result is consistent with the findings of Titman (1983). The coefficients of the transportation and wholesale-retail dummy variables are also significant in each of the five sample periods, having respectively positive and negative signs.

The explanatory power of the model is relatively low, having an R^2 that fails to exceed 10 percent in any sample period. This point is discussed at length in the conclusion to this chapter. The results presented in table 5–3, where long-term debt less cash and short-term investments has been used as a measure of debt, are very similar to those presented in table 5–1. Since the only difference of note is a systematic decline in the absolute value of the wholesale-retail dummy variable, we do not discuss these results further.

The regression model used to generate the results presented in table 5–2 includes current liabilities in the measure of the firm's debt. Use of these liabilities results in a decline in the explanatory power of the model (R^2) relative to the results presented in table 5–1. The coefficient of the firm size variable is negative in all five sample periods and significant in three of these periods. The estimated coefficient of the variability measure is significant and positive in three of the five sample periods. These results run counter to the predictions of the model. The coefficients of the depreciation and interest rate variables are not significant in this version of the empirical model. In addition, the wholesale-retail dummy variable (Dummy 3) has a positive sign in each sample period, although the estimated coefficient is never significant.

An Alternative Specification of the Regression Model

Although the results we have presented support the importance of depreciation expense and the coupon rate on long-term debt in determining financial leverage, the explanatory power of the model was rather low. The determinants of capital structure are now examined using an alternative specification of the regression model.

The theoretical model of the firm's optimal debt to total assets ratio was derived under the implicit assumption that the firm's dividend and leverage decisions are independent. This assumption is tested by including a dividend payout variable in the empirical model. While this ad hoc procedure cannot confirm any causal relationship between dividend payout and leverage, it does provide a direct test of the independence of dividend and leverage policy, a common assumption in financial economics [a notable exception is Litzenberger and Van Horne (1978)]. The dividend payout variable that has been used was calculated using the average ratio of total dividends to net operating income plus depreciation in the 3 years prior to the observation of the debt to total assets ratio.

In the regression results reported in tables 5–1 to 5–3, the proxy for the coupon rate on long-term debt was calculated using total interest expense rather than interest expense on long-term debt as required by the theoretical model. This suggests that the proxy for the coupon rate on the firm's long-term debt is likely to include a significant measurement error. Consequently, the interest rate variable has not been included in the alternative empirical model in an attempt to eliminate measurement error in the explanatory variables.

Except for the fact that a dividend payout variable has been included and the interest rate variable excluded, the explanatory variables in the regression model that is tested here are identical to those described previously. Two proxies for the debt to total assets ratio are considered here. The first is the ratio of the book value of long-term debt to the book value of total assets. The results obtained using this variable are presented in table 5–4. Note that this measure of financial leverage was also considered in table 5–1. Consequently, the alternative specification of the explanatory variables can be compared to the results of the theoretical model.

The alternative regression model (table 5–4) provides an interesting contrast to the regression model examined previously. The explanatory power of the two models is similar. In addition, both models indicate that firms in manufacturing tend to have a lower debt to total assets ratio (the dummy variable for manufacturing has a significant negative coefficient) than the average, while firms in the transportation industry tend to have more debt than the average (the dummy variable for the transportation industry is significantly positive).

The results of the two models differ with respect to the sign and significance of the firm size and depreciation variables. Table 5–4 shows the size variable to be significantly positive as predicted by the theoretical model, whereas the results obtained in table 5–1 using an empirical version of the theoretical model indicate that leverage is negatively related to firm size (although the coefficients are not statistically significant in most instances). The empirical proxy for the rate at which the firm's capital depreciates is not statistically significant in this specification of the regression model. This is in contrast to the results presented in tables 5–1 and 5–3, where the depreciation variable had a significant negative relation to financial leverage.

A proxy for the firm's dividend payout was not included in any of the theoretical versions of the regression model. The results presented in table 5–4 show a significant and positive relationship between financial leverage and dividend payout in all five sample periods. Although this statistical relationship does not imply any causal relationship between the firm's leverage and dividend decisions, the results provide evidence that financial leverage and dividend policy may be interdependent, as suggested by Litzenberger and Van Horne (1978).

The debt to total assets ratio was also calculated using the book value of debt less net working capital (current assets minus current liabilities) as a measure of the firm's debt. The rationale for the use of this measure is that current

Table 5–4
Cross-Sectional Analysis of Capital Structure with Dividend Payout Included as an Explanatory Variable

Year	Constant	Log Size	Variability	Depreciation Expense	Coupon Rate	Dummy 1	Dummy 2	Dummy 3	N	F Ratio	R^2
1976	0.146 (9.367)	0.014 (6.415)	−0.007 (1.287)	0.011 (1.414)	0.054 (3.191)	−0.022 (−1.954)	0.073 (3.671)	0.010 (0.530)	1,759	14	.051
1977	0.221 (12.228)	0.012 (5.053)	−0.033 (−5.318)	0.012 (1.253)	0.251 (5.106)	−0.047 (−3.700)	0.081 (3.624)	0.028 (1.385)	1,866	20	.069
1978	0.157 (10.371)	0.005 (6.277)	0.010 (1.825)	−0.015 (−1.766)	0.426 (8.828)	−0.037 (−3.602)	0.113 (6.277)	0.007 (0.503)	2,121	33	.097
1979	0.149 (10.582)	0.009 (4.238)	0.009 (1.702)	0.002 (0.428)	0.135 (4.321)	−0.033 (−3.278)	0.106 (5.945)	0.008 (0.560)	2,261	21	.059
1980	0.156 (12.706)	0.014 (7.495)	−0.001 (−0.317)	0.001 (1.216)	0.098 (4.137)	−0.053 (−5.834)	0.079 (4.866)	.001 (0.064)	2,286	29	.080

Notes: Dependent variable is $\dfrac{\text{Book value of long-term debt}}{\text{Total assets}}$. t statistics are in parentheses.

Table 5-5

Cross-Sectional Analysis of Capital Structure with Dividend Payout as an Explanatory Variable and Debt Reduced by Net Working Capital

Year	Constant	Log Size	Variability	Depreciation Expense	Coupon Rate	Dummy 1	Dummy 2	Dummy 3	N	F Ratio	R^2
1976	-0.081 (-3.396)	0.042 (12.541)	-0.040 (5.075)	0.026 (2.201)	0.069 (2.659)	-0.216 (-12.535)	0.131 (4.314)	-0.121 (-4.267)	1,759	68	.212
1977	-0.036 (-1.406)	-0.044 (12.872)	-0.055 (-6.226)	0.041 (3.072)	-0.015 (-0.215)	-0.240 (-13.467)	0.141 (4.521)	-0.086 (-3.058)	1,866	78	.226
1978	-0.086 (-3.838)	-0.040 (12.598)	-0.028 (-3.451)	0.022 (1.746)	0.156 (2.163)	-0.216 (-14.129)	0.195 (7.289)	-0.110 (-5.172)	2,121	94	.236
1979	-.0930 (-4.365)	0.041 (13.541)	-0.029 (-3.854)	-0.022 (2.610)	-0.014 (-0.305)	-0.210 (-13.748)	-.196 (7.282)	-0.111 (-5.159)	2,261	92	.219
1980	0.0667 (-3.109)	0.0473 (14.44)	-0.0475 (-7.218)	0.004 (1.86)	0.046 (1.103)	-0.237 (-14.756)	0.173 (6.007)	-0.132 (-5.826)	2,286	95	.224

Notes: Dependent variable is $\dfrac{\text{Book value of long-term debt} + \text{Current liabilities} - \text{Current assets}}{\text{Total assets}}$. *t* statistics are in parentheses.

liabilities are used to finance current assets (at least to some extent). An excess of current assets over current liabilities represents funds that could be used to retire long-term debt, while an excess of current liabilities over current assets may indicate that short-term borrowing (in one form or another) has been used as a substitute for long-term debt. The results obtained using this measure of the debt to total assets ratio are presented in table 5–5.

The inclusion of net working capital as an offset to long-term debt in the debt to total assets ratio improves the explanatory power of the alternative regression model by 10 percent or more in each of the cross-sectional regressions. Note that the explanatory power of this model is also greater than that of the theoretical model. One interpretation that can be given to these results is that long-term debt less net working capital reflects a firm's financial leverage position more accurately than the other measures of financial leverage that have been examined.

The coefficient of the size variable is significantly positive, and the coefficient of the variability measure is significantly negative, as is predicted by the theoretical model. Note that these coefficients appear to be relatively stable across sample periods. The coefficient of the depreciation variable is positive in each of the five sample periods, with a t statistic greater than 2 in three periods. These aspects of the results are in sharp contrast to the results presented earlier.

The effect of industry classification in this version of the regression model is consistent with the results of the theoretical model. Both the manufacturing variable (Dummy 1) and the transportation variable (Dummy 2) are significant, being respectively negative and positive. The wholesale-retail variable (Dummy 3) is significantly negative, which is consistent with the results presented in table 5–1.

Conclusion

This chapter analyzed the empirical relationship between firm size and leverage. The empirical tests that were described were based on the theoretical model developed in chapter 3. In addition, the effects of industry-specific factors that may have been omitted from the theoretical model were examined by including dummy variables denoting industrial classification in the regression equations.

The results of the empirical analysis are mixed. The explanatory power of all of the empirical models tested was relatively low. The R^2s of the regression models that were examined were never greater than 25 percent.

The results seem to be quite sensitive to the definition of the dependent variable that is used. The explanatory power of the model decreased when current liabilities were included in the definition of debt. However, the treatment of cash and short-term investments as an offset to debt seemed to have only a marginal effect on the results. The debt to total assets ratio was found to have a significant negative relationship to the rate of depreciation and the coupon rate on debt, as predicted by the model. However, the coefficients of the size and variability measures were found to be generally insignificant, having the wrong sign in many instances.

The empirical model, which included a dividend payout variable (and excluded the proxy for the coupon rate on debt), was tested. Once again, the results appeared to be sensitive to the proxy for the use of debt financing that was used. The inclusion of current assets as an offset to long-term debt plus current liabilities in the debt to total assets ratio increased the explanatory power of the model. The alternative specification of the empirical model gives results that differ dramatically from those for the theoretical model. In this case, the coefficients of the size and variability measures are significant. The effects of these variables are in the directions predicted by the theoretical model. Of further interest is the fact that the estimated values of the coefficients are relatively stable across sample periods. On the negative side, the coefficient of the depreciation variable is significantly positive in some instances, contrary to the predictions of the model.

The results confirm the significance of industry classification in predicting corporate leverage. The coefficients of the industry dummy variables for manufacturing and transportation were generally significant for each specification of the model. Manufacturing firms tended to have lower debt to total assets ratios (that is, a negative coefficient for the industry dummy variable), whereas transportation firms tended to have a higher debt to total assets ratio than average.

These results lend empirical support to the theoretical model developed in chapter 3. The fact that the evidence presented is not conclusive can be attributed, in part, to a failure to identify correctly the concept of debt that is relevant to financial managers in determining leverage. Another factor contributing to the relatively low explanatory power of the model is the effect of the net operating loss carry over provisions of the IRS Code. This provision should dilute the importance of tax shield substitutes in the determination of financial leverage policy.

The explanatory power of the model may also be related to the selection bias implicit in the database that has been used. The COMPUSTAT Industrial and OTC files include data on only firms that are very large, in relation to the median size for all businesses. Thus, an important group of firms (in particular, small businesses) has been systematically excluded from the sample. The theoretical model predicts that the most dramatic differences in the debt to total assets ratio arise between the firms in the smallest size categories. These are the very firms that are not included in the COMPUSTAT data that we used in this analysis. This suggests that even though there is wide variation in the size of the firms included in the sample, the range of firms included in the model may not be sufficiently wide to validate the theoretical model.

6

Stock Market Return and Firm Size: A Synthesis of the Explanations and Some Empirical Tests

Earlier chapters have, for the most part, analyzed accounting data. This chapter examines stock market returns of publicly traded firms. Our principal objective is to summarize and further analyze the evidence that suggests that small firms earn abnormally high returns.

In 1981, Banz[1] reported that during the past 50 years small firms on the NYSE have earned higher stock market rates of return on a risk-adjusted basis than large firms. In subsequent studies the same phenomenon has been documented for firms listed on the AMEX and OTC markets, as well as stock markets in Canada and Australia. This size effect is anomalous because it is inconsistent with efficient markets in which securities of equal risk earn equal returns. It implies that investors in small firms demand a higher risk-adjusted return than investors in large firms, and this demand results in a higher cost of capital for small firms. A differentially higher cost of capital for small firms implies that certain investments, profitable for large firms, would not be profitable for small firms.

This chapter first describes the size effect and then documents it. Second, statistical explanations of the anomalous size effect are examined. Third, variables other than size are examined as possible explanations of the size effect. In particular, the influence of financial policy—dividend policy and leverage policy—on the stock market return of small and large firms is examined.

Description of the Size Effect

The size effect is an empirical phenomenon that emerged from tests of the Sharpe (1964) and Lintner (1965) capital asset pricing model (CAPM) (hereafter called the Sharpe-Lintner model). Under the assumptions of individuals risk aversion, homogeneous beliefs, perfect capital markets,[2] Sharpe and Lintner demonstrate that

$$E(\bar{R}_j) = R_f + \beta_j[E(\bar{R}_m) - R_f], \qquad (6.1)$$

where $E(\tilde{R}_j)$ and $E(\tilde{R}_m)$ are the expected rates of return on security, j, and market portfolio, m, respectively; R_f is the riskless rate of interest; and β_j is security j's relative risk (β) coefficient. For expositional purposes, it is useful to rewrite equation (6.1) as

$$\frac{E(\tilde{R}_j) - R_f}{\beta_j} = E(\tilde{R}_m) - R_f. \tag{6.2}$$

The implication of equation (6.2) is that all risky assets in the capital market are expected to have the same risk-adjusted rate of return.

Empirical tests of the CAPM use proxy variables for $E(\tilde{R}_j)$ and β_j since they are expectational values and hence are not directly observable. Time series historical return data are averaged to provide $\tilde{R}_j$, the mean realized return, and are regressed on a time series of market index return data to provide β_j, an estimate of security j's beta. The size effect phenomenon refers to the fact that the realized risk-adjusted return for small firms (denoted by the subscript S) is significantly greater than the realized risk-adjusted return for large firms (L); that is,

$$\frac{\tilde{R}_S - R_f}{\hat{\beta}_S} > \frac{\tilde{R}_L - R_f}{\hat{\beta}_L}. \tag{6.3}$$

It should be noted that cross sectionally examining the constancy of realized risk-adjusted returns represents a valid test of the CAPM only if there is reason to believe that expectations are, on average, realized during the investigation period and that the risky return distributions are stationary through time. Only under these assumptions are the mean realized return, $\tilde{R}_j$, and the ordinary least squares (OLS) slope coefficient, $\hat{\beta}_j$, unbiased estimators of the expectational variables $E(\tilde{R}_j)$ and β_j, respectively.

Table 6A–1 summarizes some of the empirical evidence that documents the size effect. The procedures by which the various authors arrive at their results are roughly equivalent, although some important methodological differences exist that are discussed later in this chapter. At the beginning of each calendar year during the sample period, stocks are rank ordered by the dollar value of outstanding common equity and are then clustered into portfolios, usually 10 in number. Portfolio return series for that year are then computed by equal-weighted, cross-sectional averaging of each portfolio's constituent stock returns. The procedure is then repeated for each year during the sample period, resulting in 10 market value portfolio time series vectors. The mean return of each portfolio time series is computed, the riskless rate is subtracted from the mean return, and the difference is divided by an estimate of the portfolio's systematic risk. In table 6A–1, the size effect elicited from this procedure is demonstrated by presenting the average realized risk-adjusted return differentials between the smallest firm portfolio and the largest firm portfolio for a number of studies.

The return differentials are arithmetically annualized to facilitate interstudy comparisons.

The values of the return differentials in table 6A–1 should not all be thought of as independent observations of the size effect because many of the studies used data from either the Center for Research in Security Prices (CRSP) monthly or the CRSP daily returns file and because the sample periods overlap. For example, both the Banz (1981) and Stoll and Whaley (1983) studies use the CRSP monthly file that includes only NYSE stocks, and both report arithmetic average return differentials of about 12 percent. In contrast, the Reinganum (1981a, 1982), Keim (1983a), and Blume and Stambaugh (1983) studies use the CRSP daily file that also includes AMEX securities. Since the cross-sectional dispersion of market values has widened as a result of including the AMEX firms, an increased small firm/large firm return differential is reported in these studies. The Morgan, MacBeth, and Novak (1982) and Brown et al. (1983) studies indicate that the size effect is also present for Canadian and Australian stocks.

The startlingly high values of the return differentials reported in table 6A–1 have been regarded as evidence refuting the Sharpe-Lintner specification of the CAPM. The theory predicts that these values should be equal to zero, and such is not the case. On the U.S. exchanges, they range from about 12 percent using monthly data for NYSE firms to about 30 percent daily data for NYSE and AMEX firms.

Explanations of the size effect may be grouped into two categories. The first category contains studies that maintain the size effect is nothing more than a statistical artifact. The premise, in most cases, is that the realized return for small firms is overstated or that the estimated systematic risk for small firms is understated, thus producing an upward-biased measure of risk-adjusted return. Once the bias is corrected, no evidence of a size effect would remain, and the validity of the CAPM would no longer be in question. The second category contains studies that offer alternative economic explanations of the size effect. In these studies, the misspecification of the Sharpe-Lintner CAPM is accepted, but variables having more economic justification than firm size are proposed as the missing factors. Once the missing factor(s) is (are) accounted for, the risk-adjusted returns will be brought into line.

Our objective is to replicate and, in some cases, extend the work of others, seeking explanations for the size effect. The database used for our empirical analysis is described in the next section. Then statistical explanations of the size effect are considered. We conclude that biases in the measurement of return and in the risk adjustment have caused the small firm effect to be exaggerated. Nevertheless, after appropriate adjustment a small firm effect remains, most of it appearing in January of each year. The second major section examines economic factors other than systematic risk that may affect differences in stock market returns of firms. These include dividend yield and leverage. No clear explanation of the small firm effect emerges in this analysis.

Data

The data used in this study were drawn from the CRSP daily return file and from the COMPUSTAT annual industrial file. The examination period extends from 2 January 1963 through 31 December 1981–19 years in all. For a firm to be included in the sample in a given year, it had to have continuous return data available for the entire year on the CRSP file and financial statement data available for the year on the COMPUSTAT file.[3] The numbers of firms meeting the dual criteria in each of the 19 years are listed in table 6A–2. The sample size ranges from 677 in 1963 to 1,597 in 1981.[4]

To assess the magnitude of the size effect in the present sample, portfolio returns were created. At the beginning of each year during the 19-year sample period, firms were ranked into 10 portfolios.[5] Portfolio return series for each year were then computed by equal-weighted, cross-sectional averaging of the daily returns of the stocks within each portfolio. The annual rate of return for each portfolio was computed in two ways: by linking the daily returns geometrically and by summing the daily returns arithmetically. Averages of the 19 yearly rates of return of each portfolio are reported in table 6A–3.

The magnitude of the size effect is immediately obvious. Even if the arithmetic rate of return is used for evaluation, the annual rate of return between the smallest firm and largest firm portfolios is in excess of 27 percent. (With the geometric rate of return the difference is in excess of 41 percent.) The impact of each of the explanations to follow is measured in terms of its ability to reduce this return differential.

It is worthwhile to make one final note about the composition of the stock portfolios before proceeding with the explanations. Stratifying the stocks by the market value of common equity tended to cluster stocks by the exchange on which they are listed. Table 6A–4 shows that over 92 percent of the stocks in the smallest market value portfolios are listed on the AMEX, OTC, or one of the regional exchanges. At the other extreme, nearly 98 percent of the stocks in the largest market value portfolio are NYSE firms. With such the case, it is conceivable that some of the return differential between the smallest and largest firm deciles is attributable to an exchange effect.

Statistical Explanations of the Size Effect

The studies that focus on a statistical artifact explanation of the size effect can be segmented according to whether they focus on the numerator or the denominator of the risk-adjusted return measure,

$$\frac{\bar{R}_j - R_f}{\hat{\beta}_j} ; \qquad (6.4)$$

that is, the study tries to explain the size effect either by arguing that the mean realized return is systematically upward biased for small firms or by arguing that the estimated β for small firms is downward biased.

Bias in the Mean Realized Return

Three separate but related studies—Roll (1983a), Blume and Stambaugh (1983), and Roll (1984)—contribute to the explanation of why the mean realized return of small firms exceeds that of large firms. Apparently the order in which stock returns are aggregated into portfolios and through time is critical to meaningful interpretation of asset pricing tests.

Implicit in the use of equation (6.4) as a test statistic is the assumption that the length of time between the price observations used to compute return is equivalent to the length of the investor's holding period. If daily return observations are used, the investor is assumed to make his or her portfolio decisions each day. If the investor has a longer holding period, the returns must be aggregated to reflect the length of the holding period.

The two most common methods of aggregation involve a two-step procedure that begins with an equal-weighted averaging of the daily returns of the portfolio's constituent stocks and ends with a time series aggregation to the desired holding period length by geometric or arithmetic means. (These two procedures were used in table 6A–3.) Roll (1983a) labels the former method the *rebalanced* portfolio return estimator. The rebalanced portfolio return is

$$\bar{R}_{RB} = \prod_{t=1}^{T} \left(1 + \frac{1}{n} \sum_{j=1}^{n} R_{jt} \right) - 1, \qquad (6.5)$$

where n is the number of stocks in the portfolio and T is the length of the holding period measured in days. Note that equation (6.5) averages stock returns cross sectionally and then aggregates geometrically the average returns to the holding period length; that is, the portfolio is assumed to be rebalanced daily so that each day during the holding period begins with an equal dollar investment in each stock.

The second common method of aggregation is the arithmetic portfolio return,

$$\bar{R}_{AR} = \sum_{t=1}^{T} \frac{1}{n} \sum_{j=1}^{n} R_{jt}. \qquad (6.6)$$

This approach, used largely for expositional purposes, again implies daily rebalancing of the portfolio but then only approximates the portfolio's holding period return by summing the daily returns.

Investor buy-and-hold experience, however, would be more accurately captured if the time series returns for each stock were linked geometrically through time to the desired holding period length and then averaged cross sectionally to form the holding period return for the portfolio; that is,

$$R_{BH} = \frac{1}{n} \sum_{j=1}^{n} \left[\prod_{t=1}^{T} (1 + R_{jt}) - 1 \right]. \tag{6.7}$$

This estimator is the true rate of return on an equal-weighted portfolio of common stocks over a holding period of length T days.

To examine the extent of the bias created by using the rebalanced, or arithmetic, portfolio returns rather than the buy-and-hold return, assume stock returns are generated as

$$\tilde{R}_{jt} = \mu_i + \tilde{\varepsilon}_{jt}, \tag{6.8}$$

where $E(\tilde{R}_{jt}) = \mu_j$ and $E(\tilde{\varepsilon}_{jt}) = 0$. The expected values of the estimators (6.5), (6.6), and (6.7) over a 2-day interval are[6]

$$E(\tilde{R}_{RB}) = 2\bar{\mu} + \bar{\mu}^2 + \sigma_{\bar{\varepsilon}_1, \bar{\varepsilon}_2}, \tag{6.9}$$

$$E(\tilde{R}_{AR}) = 2\bar{\mu}, \tag{6.10}$$

and

$$E(\tilde{R}_{BH}) = 2\bar{\mu} + \overline{\mu^2} + \bar{\sigma}_{\varepsilon_1, \varepsilon_2}, \tag{6.11}$$

where

$$\bar{\mu} = \frac{1}{n} \sum_{j=1}^{n} \mu_j, \quad \overline{\mu^2} = \frac{1}{n} \sum_{j=1}^{n} \mu_j^2;$$

$$\bar{\varepsilon}_t = \frac{1}{n} \sum_{j=1}^{n} \varepsilon_{jt};$$

$$\sigma_{\bar{\varepsilon}_1, \bar{\varepsilon}_2} = \text{covariance} \left(\frac{1}{n} \sum_{j=1}^{n} \varepsilon_{j1}, \frac{1}{n} \sum_{j=1}^{n} \varepsilon_{j2} \right), \text{ the first-order serial covariance of the portfolio returns;}$$

$$\bar{\sigma}_{\varepsilon_1, \varepsilon_2} = \frac{1}{n} \sum_{j=1}^{n} \sigma_{\varepsilon_{j1}, \varepsilon_{j2}}, \text{ the average of the first-order serial covariance of individual security returns.}$$

The differences between the expected values of the respective portfolio holding period return estimators are

$$E(\bar{R}_{RB}) - E(\bar{R}_{AR}) = \bar{\mu}^2 + \sigma_{\bar{\varepsilon}_1,\bar{\varepsilon}_2}, \tag{6.12}$$

$$E(\bar{R}_{RB}) - E(\bar{R}_{BH}) = \sigma_{\bar{\varepsilon}_1,\bar{\varepsilon}_2} - \bar{\sigma}_{\varepsilon_1,\varepsilon_2} - \sigma_\mu^2, \tag{6.13}$$

and

$$E(\bar{R}_{AR}) - E(\bar{R}_{BH}) = -\overline{\mu^2} - \bar{\sigma}_{\varepsilon_1,\varepsilon_2}, \tag{6.14}$$

where $\sigma_\mu^2 = \overline{\mu^2} - \bar{\mu}^2$.

Before interpreting the degree of bias in the estimators and examining some sample estimates of the values, it is worthwhile to note two points. First, the buy-and-hold estimator is the correct measure of the holding period return of the portfolio. It is precisely the rate of return an investor would earn if he invested an equal dollar amount in each of the n stocks in the portfolio at the beginning of the holding period and held the portfolio for T days. Second, the expected values of the estimators [that is, expressions (6.9), (6.10), and (6.11)] and the degrees of bias [that is, expressions (6.12), (6.13), and (6.14)] apply only to a 2-day holding period. For longer holding periods, additional serial covariance terms appear. A T-day holding period requires serial covariance terms from order 1 to order $T - 1$. For present discussion, however, the focus is on first-order serial covariances,

$E(\bar{R}_{RB}) - E(\bar{R}_{AR})$. The expected values of the rebalanced and the arithmetic estimators are given in table 6A–3. They indicate that $E(\bar{R}_{RB})$ always exceeds $E(\bar{R}_{AR})$. As shown in expression (6.12), this is due to two factors. First, the square of the average expected stock returns, $\bar{\mu}^2$, is unambiguously positive. Second, the first-order serial covariance of portfolio returns, $\sigma_{\bar{\varepsilon}_1,\bar{\varepsilon}_2}$, tends to be positive because of infrequent trading. On any given day, certain stocks within the portfolio may not trade and will have zero returns. A day or two later when these stocks finally do trade, nonzero daily returns are recorded, reflecting, in part, a market movement that occurred a day or two beforehand. This phenomenon induces positive serial covariance in the portfolio return series as first noted by Fisher (1966). Estimated first-order serial covariance of the portfolio return series are reported in the next to last column of table 6A–5 for the 10 portfolios formed on the basis of total market value of common stocks. Note that the average portfolio serial covariance is positive for all portfolio return series. Furthermore, the higher serial covariances for the smaller firm portfolios reflect the fact that infrequent trading is a more serious problem for small firms than for large firms. The serial covariance for the smallest firm portfolio is more than twice as high as that of the largest firm portfolio.

$E(\bar{R}_{RB}) - E(\bar{R}_{BH})$. The difference between the expected values of the rebalanced and the buy-and-hold estimators, (6.13), is the first-order serial covariance in the portfolio return series less the average of the first-order serial covariances of the constitutent stock return series less the cross-sectional variance of the expected rates of return of the stocks within the portfolio. By virtue of the infrequent trading phenomenon, the first term is positive. By virtue of the fact that variance cannot be negative, the last term is positive. The magnitude and the sign of the middle term depend on the first-order serial covariances in the stock return series.

Negative first-order serial covariance in a stock return series can result from random movement from the bid price to the ask price and vice versa. To see this, assume that the true price (value) of a stock is constant through time. If an investor wishes to buy the stock, he or she must pay a price above the true price (the ask price) to compensate the market maker for providing immediacy of exchange. If an investor wishes to sell the stock, he or she must sell at a price below the true price (the bid price), again, to compensate the market maker. Now, suppose that the closing prices of a stock on successive days alternate from a bid to an ask to a bid and so on. The first-order serial covariance of the price change series would be $-s^2$, where s is the bid-ask spread. However, because the closing prices do not strictly alternate from a bid to an ask on successive days or vice versa and because the bid price and the ask are equally likely to be the closing price on a given day, the first-order serial covariance is on order of $-1/2s^2$. This result was first noted by Roll (1984).

The difference between the rebalanced and buy-and-hold portfolio estimators then becomes an empirical issue. The positive portfolio serial covariance and the negative average stock serial covariance contribute to the rebalanced estimator being larger than the buy-and-hold estimator, while the cross-sectional variance of the expected rates of return on the stocks suggests the opposite. Estimates of each of the terms are included in table 6A–5. The sum of the terms is included in the last column of the table. Note that the average first-order serial covariance in the stock returns is negative for the smallest market value portfolio.[7] The average first-order serial covariance of stock returns surprisingly is positive for the six largest portfolios for reasons that are not immediately obvious.

The net effect of the covariance and variance terms leads the rebalanced portfolio return estimator to be larger than the buy-and-hold portfolio return estimator for the eight smallest portfolios. The negative serial covariance of the stock returns for the small firms swamp the other terms in the expression. However, the values in table 6A–5 are intended only to be illustrative since higher-order covariance terms will also play a role for holding periods in excess of 2 days.

Table 6A–6 contains the average annual rates of return for the rebalanced and buy-and-hold estimators for various holding period assumptions. The basic data underlying the returns in table 6A–6 are daily returns, which are used to calculate $\bar{R}_{RB}$ and $\bar{R}_{BH}$ for each holding period according to equations (6.5) and

(6.7). These portfolio holding period returns are then annualized by compounding the appropriate number of times. If the holding period is 1 day, the rebalanced and the buy-and-hold return estimators are the same, and the small-firm/large-firm portfolio return differential is (.50277 − .08963) = 41.3 percent on an annualized basis. If, however, the investor's holding period is longer than 1 day, the rebalanced estimator calculated from daily returns is no longer a valid measure of buy-and-hold return. If the investor's holding period is 3 months, the buy-and-hold return estimates indicate that the return differential is reduced to (.30203 − .08381) = 21.8 percent. For a 1-year holding period, the smallest-firm/largest-firm return differential is about 20.96 percent, substantially less than the 41.3 percent differential based on the rebalanced estimate.

$E(\bar{R}_{AR}) − E(\bar{R}_{BH})$. Finally, the difference between the arithmetic and the buy-and-hold estimators is examined. Expression (6.14) shows that there are offsetting influences in the degree of bias in $\bar{R}_{AR}$. On one hand, the mean of the squared expected stock returns causes the arithmetic estimator to be less than the buy-and-hold estimator. On the other hand, the negative serial covariance in the stock return series causes the arithmetic estimator to be greater than the buy-and-hold estimator. If the average annual arithmetic return in table 6A–5 is contrasted with the average annual buy-and-hold return in table 6A–6, then the arithmetic return for the smallest firm portfolio is larger than the buy-and-hold return (35.2 percent versus 29.7 percent) and the arithmetic return for the largest firm portfolio is smaller than the buy-and-hold return (8.1 percent versus 8.7 percent). The return differential using the arithmetic estimator, 27 percent, thus overstates the true magnitude of the return differential, 20.96 percent, measured by the buy-and-hold estimate. The buy-and-hold differential of 20.96 percent is still quite large when compared with the results of Banz (1981) (see table 6A–1), but this is due to the fact that AMEX and some OTC firms are included, whereas the Banz study examined only NYSE firms.

Holding Period. Table 6A–6 illustrates the fact that the magnitude of the small firm effect depends on the frequency with which investors rebalance portfolios. If the investor trades securities daily, the 1-day buy-and-hold estimate yielding a return differential of (.50277 − .08963) = 41.314 percent is appropriate. If the investor trades securities annually, the annual buy-and-hold estimator yielding a return differential of (.29670 − .08710) = 20.960 percent is appropriate. Thus, the magnitude of the small firm effect depends on the investor's holding period.

Stoll and Whaley (1983) have shown that, for NYSE stocks, the minimum holding period for which transaction costs (bid-ask spread plus two commissions) are just covered is approximately 4 months. This implies that small-firm/large-firm return differentials based on holding periods of less than 4 months are inappropriate. Holding periods may, of course, be substantially greater.

We estimate the average length of the investors' holding periods by using data on the number of shares outstanding and the number of shares traded for each stock in each year.[8] Assuming the frequency of trading of a particular stock is constant through time, the holding period for that stock can be approximated using the ratio,

$$\frac{\text{number of shares outstanding}_j}{\text{number of shares traded}_j}.$$

This ratio was computed for each stock within each portfolio in each year. The ratios for the stocks within each portfolio were averaged,

$$\frac{1}{n} \sum_{j=1}^{n} \frac{\text{number of shares outstanding}_j}{\text{number of shares traded}_j},$$

in each year, then the averages were averaged across the 19 years in the sample period. The results are reported in the column labeled Stocks (Shares) in table 6A–7.

Two other estimators of holding period length were also considered because the first measure is very sensitive to outliers created by stocks that traded infrequently during a particular year. The second estimator was computed by dividing the total number of shares outstanding for the entire portfolio by the total number of shares traded,

$$\frac{\sum_{j=1}^{n} \text{number of shares outstanding}_j}{\sum_{j=1}^{n} \text{number of shares traded}_j},$$

and the third estimator was computed by dividing the total market value of the portfolio by the market value of the shares traded,

$$\frac{\sum_{j=1}^{n} \text{number of shares outstanding}_j \times \text{price per share}_j}{\sum_{j=1}^{n} \text{number of shares traded}_j \times \text{price per share}_j}.$$

The average values across the 19 years in the sample are reported in the columns labeled Portfolio (Shares) and Portfolio (Value) in table 6A–7, respectively.

These ratios are subject to some measurement problems. For example, reported share volume depends significantly on the degree of dealer intervention. For actively traded stocks two investors can trade 100 shares directly, and a volume of 100 is reported. For inactively traded stocks, investors on each side are more likely to trade through a dealer, with the result that a volume of 200 is reported. Thus, volume tends to be overstated for small companies, and this understates investors' holding periods for small companies. With respect to the measure of shares outstanding, problems may arise with respect to the appropriate method for treating closely held shares. Nevertheless, these estimators of holding period will be helpful in determining an appropriate holding period for measuring the small firm effect.

The results reported in table 6A–7 demonstrates the first estimator's sensitivity to outliers. The second and third estimators are less susceptible to such error and provide surprisingly consistent results. The smallest firms appear to be held for about 3 years on average. The holding period remains at about that same level for the next 7 portfolios, with portfolios 9 and 10 having holding periods of about 5 and 8 years, respectively. It appears that small- and middle-sized stocks trade with about the same frequency of trade and that large-sized firms trade relatively less, probably as a result of having a largely institutional clientele.

It is evident from table 6A–7 that holding period estimates exceed 2 years while the longest holding period examined in table 6A–6 was 1 year. In table 6A–8 the average 3-year rates of return using the rebalanced, arithmetic, and buy-and-hold portfolio return estimators are reported to see if the size effect is further diminished by using a lengthier holding period. The results indicate that the size effect return differential stabilizes. The annualized buy-and-hold return differential between the smallest and largest portfolios is

$$\sqrt[3]{2.13340} - \sqrt[3]{1.24082} = .212,$$

approximately the same as the annual differential in table 6A–6. The biases in the rebalanced portfolio return continue to grow.

Bias in the Systematic Risk Estimate

The β coefficient estimated using daily return data may be biased for two reasons—thin trading and return seasonality. This section addresses each of these issues.

Thin Trading. Ordinary least squares estimation of

$$R_{jt} = \alpha_j + \beta_j R_{mt} + \varepsilon_{jt} \tag{6.15}$$

on historical return data assumes that the observations of R_{jt} and R_{mt} are contemporaneous, and such a condition is seldom met in practice. On the one hand, the closing price reported for a particular stock on a given day is the price recorded at the time of the last transaction. The closing level of the stock index, on the other hand, can be thought of as taking place at an average of the times of the last transactions of all stocks. To the extent that the time of stock j's last transaction is different from the average time of the last stock index transaction, the estimator, β_j, in the preceding regression will be inconsistent.

Scholes and Williams (1977) develop a consistent estimator of β assuming that each stock is traded at least once during the day and that the stock and the stock index prices are nonsynchronous. Their estimator is

$$\beta_j = \frac{(\beta_j^{-1} + \beta_j^0 + \beta_j^{+1})}{(1 + 2\rho_1)}, \tag{6.16}$$

where β_j^{-1}, β_j^0, and β_j^{+1} are coefficients from the simple linear regressions of R_{jt} on the lagged, R_{mt-1}, the contemporaneous, R_{mt}, and the leading, R_{mt+1}, market returns respectively. The parameter, ρ_1, is the first-order serial correlation coefficient in the market return series. Unfortunately, the Scholes-Williams estimator does not account for the fact that some stocks are so thinly traded that a stock transaction may not occur at all in a given day. In fact, for many stocks traded on the NYSE and the AMEX, there may be no transaction for several days.

Dimson (1979) attempts to develop an estimator that incorporates this infrequent trading phenomenon. His estimator, labeled the *aggregated coefficient method*, sums the slope coefficients on the time series multiple regression,

$$R_{jt} = \alpha_j + \sum_{i=-n}^{n} \beta_j^i R_{mt+i} + \varepsilon_{jt}, \tag{6.17}$$

to obtain a consistent estimator of the β for stock j. Recently, however, Fowler and Rorke (1983) demonstrate that this approach is incorrect and that the consistent estimator of systematic risk under the thin trading phenomenon is

$$\beta_j = \sum_{i=-n}^{n} \beta_j^i \bigg/ \left(1 + 2 \sum_{i=1}^{n} \rho_i\right), \tag{6.18}$$

where β_j^i is the coefficient from the simple linear regression of R_{jt} on R_{mt-i} and ρ_i is the ith-order serial correlation coefficient in the market return series. Note that, where n equals 1, the corrected Dimson estimator becomes the Scholes-Williams estimator.

The first author to suggest that the size effect may be attributable to infrequent trading was Roll (1981). His argument is that small firms are less frequently traded than large firms; hence, the systematic risk coefficient estimated from the ordinary least squares regression of (6.15) will be more downward biased for small firms than large firms.

To test Roll's conjecture about the frequency of trading of small firms versus large firms, the number of zero daily stock returns in the sample was counted. Since a zero return may indicate that no trade took place or that the price remained unchanged from the previous day, the number of zero returns is an upward-biased estimate of trading frequency. However, for the purpose of determining relative trading frequency, the estimate should be adequate. Table 6A–9 contains a summary of the zero return frequency results. Inspection of table 6A–9 shows that nearly 35 percent of the daily stock returns in the smallest market value portfolio were zero returns and that just under 12 percent of the daily stock returns in the largest market value portfolio were zeros.[9] Thus, large firms appear to trade three times as often as small firms. This evidence supports, at least indirectly, Roll's notion of less frequent trading of the stocks of small firms.

The magnitude of the bias in the systematic risk coefficient is assessed by Reinganum (1982). Using daily returns, he finds that the OLS estimator of systematic risk of the smallest firm portfolio is .75 as compared to 1.69 when the Dimson estimator is used. Stoll and Whaley (1983) show there is little difference between the OLS and Dimson estimators when monthly returns are used. However, interpretation of these results is tenuous because the Dimson estimator has been shown to be inconsistent. We now turn to a second source of bias—weekly seasonality in returns—and then present estimators of systematic risk that overcome both sources of bias.

Stock Return Seasonality. French (1980) and Gibbons and Hess (1981) document a pronounced weekly seasonality in stock returns. More specifically, they note that the rate of return on Mondays is usually negative and that the rate of return on Fridays is slightly higher than on other days of the trading week.[10] In any case, both studies are able to reject the hypothesis that the rates of return for the days during the trading week are equal; hence, the OLS regression model (6.15), as well as the corrected aggregated coefficients method (6.18), are misspecified. The systematic risk coefficients will be biased as a result of the missing variables being correlated with the market returns.

To illustrate the day-of-the-week effect and to examine whether it is different for small firms than for large firms, the average rates of return by trading day were computed. The daily returns were arithmetically annualized to facilitate interpretation. The results are reported in table 6A–10.

Consistent with the results of French and Gibbons and Hess the average rate of return on Monday is negative; however, it is more negative for large firms than small firms. Conversely, the average rate of return on Friday for small firms is considerably greater than it is for large firms. Without pursuing the day-of-the-week discussion any further, it would be reasonable to conclude that there is considerable margin for error in estimating systematic risk coefficients from daily data, even if an aggregated coefficients method is used.

For this reason, the systematic risk coefficients in this study were estimated using weekly returns. The daily rates of return for each stock were geometrically aggregated to the week's end and were recorded. Note that in using weekly returns, not only is the daily seasonal removed, but also the infrequent trading phenomenon is reduced. As a result, fewer leading and lagged market returns are necessary in the aggregated coefficients computation.

Estimating Systematic Risk Coefficients. To estimate systematic risk coefficients of portfolios, the portfolio return series is generated by equal weighting the portfolio's constituent stock return series—that is,

$$R_{pt} = \frac{1}{n} \sum_{j=1}^{n} R_{jt},\qquad(6.19)$$

for $t = 1, \ldots, T$. These portfolio returns are regressed on the returns of the CRSP value-weighted market index. The results of the OLS market model regressions (6.15) on weekly portfolio returns are reported in the third column of table 6A–11.

For the smallest firm portfolio, the systematic risk estimate is .989, and for the largest firm portfolio it is .999. While it is expected that the largest firm portfolio has a systematic risk estimate near one, the risk estimates for the smaller firm portfolios, particularly portfolios 1 and 2 (see table 6A–11), appear to be substantially understated.

Although the infrequent trading problem is reduced when weekly returns are used in place of daily returns, it is doubtful that the return observations of the portfolio and the market are synchronous so that the Scholes-Williams estimator using one leading and one lagged variable is more appropriate than the simple OLS market model. As an additional check, the aggregated coefficient estimator (6.18) was also computed using two leading and two lagged variables. The results are reported for each of the portfolio return series in the last two columns in table 6A–11.

It is interesting to note that using only one leading and one lagged variable did not fully capture the additional systematic risk attributable to the infrequent trading of the smaller firms. The two leading and two lagged variables appear to do a better job.

In summary, the biases associated with computation of mean realized return and with estimation of systematic risk have been examined and evaluated empirically. Using a 1-year holding period as a reasonable estimate of the investor's investment horizon, table 6A–12 describes the size effect after the statistical problems are corrected. The average annual return column is that computed using the buy-and-hold portfolio estimator. The systematic risk estimate is the aggregated coefficient using two leading and two lagged market return variables. The average risk-adjusted return is the annual portfolio return less the riskless rate divided by the systematic risk coefficient [that is, expression (6.4)]. The risk-adjusted return differential between the smallest firm and the largest firm portfolio is still 18.7 percent on an annualized basis. This amount is considerably less than the risk-adjusted return differentials reported by other studies that used the CRSP daily return file and included AMEX stocks. However, it remains disturbingly large.

Economic Explanations

The economic explanations of the size effect focus on identifying a missing factor in the Sharpe-Lintner CAPM. While some authors suggest that size is the missing variable, most argue that size is merely a surrogate for some other factor or set of factors. Missing factors that have been suggested are dividend yield, earnings yield, transaction costs, alternate risk measures, investor preference for higher-order moments of the return distribution, differential information, and industry effects. The focus in this book is on variables reflecting a firm's financial policy. In particular, dividend yield, earnings yield, and debt-equity ratios are evaluated as explanations of the size effect. In addition, the role of transaction costs is examined. The section begins with the Sharpe-Lintner model and the size effect recast in the form of a cross-sectional regression of stock return on its underlying determinants.

The CAPM

Consider the cross-sectional regression of realized annual risk premium on systematic risk,

$$R_j - R_f = \gamma_0 + \gamma_1 \hat{\beta}_j + \varepsilon_j, \tag{6.20}$$

where R_j is annual realized return on stock j, R_f is the riskless rate of return, $\hat{\beta}_j$ is an estimate of stock j's systematic risk, and ε_j is a random disturbance term. Regression model (6.20) is the ex post version of the Sharpe-Lintner CAPM (6.1), and if expectations are on average realized, the values of γ_0 and γ_1 should be zero and $R_m - R_f$, respectively.

The cross-sectional results of regression (6.20) for each of the 19 years in the sample period are reported in table 6A–13. On average, they may be interpreted as modest support in favor of the Sharpe-Lintner model. The intercept term is, on average, not significantly different from zero, while the null hypothesis of a zero slope term may be rejected. At first glance, the violent swings of the yearly slope term estimates from positive to negative may seem to be a source of concern. However, one must recall that regression (6.20) represents a valid test of the Sharpe-Lintner model only if there is reason to believe expectations were realized. Casual inspection of the market returns reported in table 6A–14 reveals that in many years the realized rate of return for the market is below the riskless rate of interest. These are clearly cases in which expectations were not realized. The overall average of the slope term is .05465, however. If the Sharpe-Lintner model term is correct and if expectations were realized on average over the 19-year period, this number represents the market risk premium and should compare reasonably well with the values reported in table 6A–14.

On the basis of the data in table 6A–14, the average realized risk premium for the Standard & Poor's 500 Index is $-.01339$, for the CRSP value-weighted index it is .03412, and for the CRSP equal-weighted index it is .16637. These figures stand to reason. The manner in which the slope coefficient is estimated implies that each of the stocks is weighted equally in the determination of the market return. Because small firms tend to have higher realized rates of return than large firms, the estimated market return from the regression should exceed the realized returns of the value-weighted indexes, and such is the case on average. In contrast, due to the constraints imposed on the sample data,[11] the sample firms will be a subset of those used to compute the CRSP equal-weighted index, and that subset will tend to consist of larger firms. Again, due to the size effect, the estimated return from the regression will tend to be less than the CRSP equal-weighted index return.

Now, consider the cross-sectional regression of realized annual return on systematic risk and total market value of common stock,

$$R_j - R_f = \gamma_0 + \gamma_1\hat{\beta}_j + \gamma_2 S_j + \varepsilon_j, \qquad (6.21)$$

where S_j is the total market value of common stock. If the Sharpe-Lintner model is correctly specified, the coefficient γ_2 should not be different from zero. As evidenced by the results reported in table 6A–15, such is not the case. While the intercept and slope estimates $\hat{\gamma}_0$ and $\hat{\gamma}_1$ do not change appreciably, the estimate of $\hat{\gamma}_2$ is, on average, negative, confirming the presence of a size effect.

It is interesting to note that in 6 of the 19 regressions, $\hat{\gamma}_2$ is positive. This result, as noted by Brown, Kleidon, and Marsh (1983), indicates that the size effect is not stationary through time and that, on occasion, there is a premium paid for large firms.

Dividend Yield

Defense for the inclusion of a dividend yield variable in the cross-sectional tests of the CAPM arises from the fact that investors pay one tax on dividend or interest income and another rate, usually lower, on capital gains income. Brennan (1970b) derives the mean variance CAPM under this scenario and finds that the structure of capital asset returns is

$$E(\bar{R}_j) = R_f + \beta_j [E(\bar{R}_m) - R_f - T(d_m - R_f)] + T(d_j - R_j), \qquad (6.22)$$

where d_j and d_m are the dividend yields of stock j and the market portfolio, respectively, and T is the ratio of the weighted average of investor tax rates on dividend (T_d) and capital gains (T_g) income, $(T_d - T_g)/(1 - T_g)$. To illustrate the sign and approximate magnitude of T, consider the case where all individuals pay a 50 percent tax rate on dividend income and a 20 percent tax rate on capital gains. The value of T would be .375. In light of the preferential tax treatment of capital gains, individuals will demand more before-tax return the higher is a stock's dividend yield, systematic risk remaining constant.

Prior to the discovery of the size effect, the empirical support of the after-tax version of the CAPM was mixed. Brennan (1970a), Litzenberger and Ramaswamy (1979), and Blume (1980) found that dividend yield is a significantly positive determinant of the observed structure of stock returns, while Black and Scholes (1974) and Miller and Scholes (1982) found that it is not. The cross-sectional regression results of the ex post version of the Brennan model,

$$R_j - R_f = \gamma_0 + \gamma_1 \hat{\beta}_j + \hat{\gamma}_2(d_j - R_f), \qquad (6.23)$$

reported in table 6A–16 indicate that $\hat{\gamma}_2$ is, on average, positive but not significantly different from zero.

Recently, Cook and Rozeff (1982) and Keim (1983b) have rekindled interest in dividend yield as a possible explainer of the size effect even though, a priori, there is little reason to believe that dividend yield and firm size should be strongly correlated. One plausible hypothesis is that small firms find it relatively more costly than large firms to raise funds externally and, therefore, retain a greater proportion of earnings to finance new investment. Hence, small firms would tend to have lower dividend yields. However, this cannot be an explanation for the small firm effect since low dividend yield tends to be associated with low expected returns. For dividend yield to be the missing factor, it would have to be strongly negatively correlated with firm size, and such is not the case. The correlation coefficients reported in table 6A–17 are positive in all but one of the 19 periods and are significantly different from zero in only 7 of the 19 periods.

Table 6A–18 contains the cross-sectional regression results of the Brennan (1970a) model when the size factor is included as an additional explanatory variable. The evidence indicates that dividend yield does little in explaining the cross-sectional variation of stock risk premiums or in dampening the size effect.

Earnings Yield

While a theoretical model that incorporates earnings yield (E/P) as an explanatory variable of stock returns has not been developed, some investigators claim that it should be a significantly positive determinant. Basu (1977), for example, investigates this hypothesis using a sample of NYSE firms during the period 1956 through 1971. He finds that during the period low earnings yield firms did outperform high earnings yield firms on a risk-adjusted basis. The cross-sectional regressions of

$$R_j - R_f = \gamma_0 + \gamma_1\hat{\beta}_j + \gamma_2 e_j + \varepsilon_j, \tag{6.24}$$

where e_j is the earnings yield of stock j, indicate likewise. The numbers reported in table 6A–19 reveal that earnings yield is a consistently positive determinant of realized risk premium. It does not appear to be related to systematic risk since the level of the market risk premium, $\hat{\gamma}_1$, and its significance in determining stock risk premium remain at about the same level as in the earlier tests.

Whether earnings yield is separate from size in explaining return is an empirical question. Reinganum (1981a) compares the two effects and finds that once the size effect is accounted for, no earnings yield effect remains. Basu (1983), however, argues that the Reinganum study has certain methodological deficiencies that, when corrected, reveal that the earnings yield effect dominates the size effect.

Table 6A–20 contains the results of a preliminary investigation on the relationship between the two factors. The correlation between earnings yield and size is not predictable in its sign and is significantly different from zero at the 5 percent level in only 1 of the 19 years. This indicates that these are probably two separable effects on return.

To test this proposition, the ex post Sharpe-Lintner model with earnings yield and size included as additional explanatory variables,

$$R_j - R_f = \gamma_0 + \gamma_1\hat{\beta}_j + \gamma_2 e_j + \gamma_3 S_j + \varepsilon_j, \tag{6.25}$$

was estimated. The results, reported in table 6A–21, indicate that there are indeed two separate effects. Earnings yield is a significantly positive determinant, while size remains a significantly negative determinant.

Debt-Equity Ratio

A firm's capital structure affects the expected rate of return on the firm's common stock indirectly through the stock's systematic risk coefficient. Hamada (1969) and Rubinstein (1973) integrate the corporate valuation work of Modigliani and Miller (1958, 1963) and demonstrate that

$$\beta_{S_j} = \beta_{V_j}[1 + (1 - t)D_j], \tag{6.26}$$

where β_{S_j} is the systematic risk coefficient of firm j's stock, β_{V_j} is the systematic risk coefficient of firm j, t is the corporate income tax rate, and D_j is the debt-equity ratio of firm j expressed in market value. The intuition underlying equation (6.26) is that the risk of the common stock is the sum of the business risk of the firm as reflected by β_{V_j} and the financial risk associated with leverage as reflected by D_j. The higher the firm's debt-equity ratio, the greater the risk faced by shareholders, β_{S_j}, and, hence, the higher the rate of return demanded by shareholders as seen through the Sharpe-Lintner model (6.1).

To begin the investigation of the effect of financial leverage on stock returns, the relationship (6.26) was tested using the cross-sectional regression,

$$\beta_j = \gamma_0 + \gamma_1 D_j + \varepsilon_j. \tag{6.27}$$

If the estimate of the firm's systematic risk is reasonably accurate, the coefficient γ_1 should be strongly positive, reflecting the association between systematic risk and leverage. If the relationship is not strongly significant, the estimated β may not be fully accounting for the financial risk faced by shareholders, and the debt-equity ratio should be included as an additional risk variable in the Sharpe-Lintner model.

The tests results of regression model (6.27) are reported in table 6A–22. The relationship between systematic risk and the debt-equity ratio is certainly not predictable. For example, in 1968 there is a significantly negative relationship at the 1 percent probability level, while in 1975 there is a significantly positive relationship at the 1 percent probability level. Overall the relationship appears negative, but not significantly so.

Since the results of table 6A–22 indicate that the estimate of systematic risk for the stock may not be fully accounting for leverage, the ex post Sharpe-Lintner model with debt-equity ratio included as an additional explanatory variable,

$$R_j - R_f = \gamma_0 + \gamma_1 \hat{\beta}_j + \gamma_2 D_j + \varepsilon_j, \tag{6.28}$$

was tested. Table 6A–23 contains a summary of the regression results. The debt-equity ratio displays only modest success in explaining stock returns. Overall the coefficient is positive and significant at the 10 percent level. The sign of the coefficient, like that of the size variable in table 6A–15, is not consistent from year to year.

For the debt-equity ratio to be the missing factor in the CAPM requires that firm size and the debt-equity ratio are negatively correlated. This requirement is counterintuitive, however, since one would expect large firms to have stabler income streams and, hence, to have greater debt capacity. The results in table 6A–24 indicate that the relationship between firm size and debt-equity is consistently negative. This relationship may be spurious since the market value of equity appears as the dependent variable and in the denominator of the independent variable.

Table 6A–25 contains a summary of the cross-sectional regression results of

$$R_j - R_f = \gamma_0 + \gamma_1 \hat{\beta}_j + \gamma_2 D_j + \gamma_3 S_j + \varepsilon_j, \tag{6.29}$$

where debt-equity and size are included as additional explanatory variables in the Sharpe-Lintner model. The evidence indicates that there are two separable effects on return, with the size effect remaining as strongly negative as it was in the outset of the investigation of the economic explanations. The coefficient of debt-equity is positive in 12 of the 19 years and is positive but insigificant on average. Financial leverage apparently is not the cause of the size effect phenomenon.

Transaction Costs

Stoll and Whaley (1983) argue that the returns of small firms are higher than the returns of large firms as a result of higher transaction costs. For investors to earn the apparently higher risk-adjusted returns of the small firms, they would have to pay proportionally higher transaction costs, both in the form of the bid-ask spread and commissions. Once these costs are imposed, the size effect disappears, at least for holding periods of less than 1 year.

Stoll and Whaley (1983) present two types of evidence in support of their hypothesis. First, they cite evidence that the percentage bid-ask spread is an inverse function of share price. Since price per share and total market value of common equity are strongly positively correlated, it may be the case that size is a direct proxy for share price that, in turn, is an inverse proxy for transaction costs. To test this hypothesis they repeat the test methodology twice, once using price per share as the stratification variable and once using size as the stratification variable. They find that the return differential between the low share price portfolio and the high share price portfolio is 0.84 percent monthly, as compared to 1 percent when size is used as the stratification variable. From this evidence they conclude that a share price effect, almost as strong as the size effect, exists.

The second type of evidence Stoll and Whaley (1983) present involves computing after-transaction-cost, risk-adjusted returns. Obviously this type of analysis is sensitive to the length of the holding period, and they begin by assuming it is 1 month in length. With a 1-month holding period and reasonable estimates of transaction cost rates, they find that the size effect is reversed: small firms have lower risk-adjusted returns than large firms. For holding periods of approximately 4 months, the abnormal risk-adjusted return for the small firm portfolio is about zero, and for holding periods from 4 months to 1 year, the abnormal risk-adjusted return of the small firm portfolio is positive but insignificant. The evidence presented in the Stoll and Whaley study, then, suggests that transaction costs may be the missing factor in the risk-return relationship.

Direct transaction costs such as the bid-ask spread and commissions for our sample of NYSE, AMEX, OTC, and regional exchange firms were too costly to collect, so the focus of the transaction cost analysis was on the determinants of transaction costs. The first one considered was price per share. As noted by Stoll and Whaley the percentage bid-ask spread is an inverse function of price so perhaps size is merely acting as a proxy for transaction costs through its correlation with price per share.

To test this proposition, realized risk premiums were regressed on systematic risk and price per share,

$$R_j - R_f = \gamma_0 + \gamma_1 \hat{\beta}_j + \gamma_2 P_j + \varepsilon_j . \qquad (6.30)$$

The results reported in table 6A–26 indicate that price per share does marginally better than size in explaining returns (see table 6A–15). Also, note that the magnitude of $\hat{\gamma}_1$ is largely the same in magnitude and significance as the regression in which size was the additional independent variable.

Table 6A–27 contains a summary of the simple correlation coefficients between price per share and size in each of the years of the sample. As expected, they are significantly positive.

Table 6A–28 contains the regression results when both price per share and size are included as explanatory variables, in the following regression:

$$R_j - R_f = \gamma_0 + \gamma_1 \hat{\beta}_j + \gamma_2 P_j + \gamma_3 S_j + \varepsilon_j . \qquad (6.31)$$

A surprising result is that, while the coefficient of price per share remains at about the same level of magnitude as in table 6A–22 where size was not included, the coefficient of size indicates that size has a positive influence on returns; that is, the introduction of price per share reverses the sign of the size effect. While this result is also puzzling, it suggests that factors related to secondary market transaction costs are relevant in explaining the size and price effects.

Conclusion

After adjusting for statistical biases in the calculation of average returns and in the calculations of the systematic risk measure, a difference of about 19 percent per year remains between the average risk-adjusted return of the smallest decile of AMEX and NYSE firms and the largest decile. Thus, while faulty statistical procedures can explain part of the small firm effect, they cannot explain it all.

A variety of economic factors that might explain cross-sectional differences in return were examined. These included systematic risk, firm size, dividend yield, earnings yield, debt-equity ratio, and factors related to secondary market transaction costs. Consistent with the evidence on the small firm effect presented earlier, firm size is a significant variable in explaining cross-sectional differences in returns even when systematic risk is also included in the regression.

Dividend yield is not a significant variable in explaining cross-sectional differences in returns, and the presence of the dividend yield variable in the cross-sectional regression does not reduce the significance of the size variable on the risk variable. While small firms tend to have lower dividend yields than large firms, dividend yield has no independent effect on realized returns.

Consistent with earlier studies, earnings yield has an independent and positive effect on average return. However, the inclusion of earnings yield does not eliminate the significance of the size variable, and the earnings yield cannot therefore be considered an explanation of the small firm effect because smaller firms continue to have higher returns. To the extent that smaller firms have higher earnings yields, small firms' returns are even higher.

Another important variable subject to a firm's control is its degree of leverage. Leverage, measured by the ratio of long-term debt to market value of equity, has a positive, marginally significant effect on realized return in a cross-sectional regression that also includes systematic risk and firm size. The inclusion of a leverage measure does not reduce the significance of the size variable and therefore cannot explain the small firm effect. The positive coefficient on leverage suggests that leverage may measure components of risk not fully reflected in the measure of systematic risk.

There is some evidence that differences in economic variables such as earnings yield and leverage may explain differences in stock market returns. However, none of these economic variables eliminates the effect of firm size.

Finally, the effect of secondary market transaction costs on stock market returns is examined. There is evidence that investors in small firms face higher transaction costs than investors in large firms and therefore demand higher before-transaction-cost returns. There is also evidence that transactions in low-price stocks incur higher transaction costs. Since there is a tendency for small firms to have low-price shares, it is possible that abnormal returns are due to low price and not to size of the firm. A cross-sectional regression including systematic risk, price per share, and firm size as independent variables substantiated this conjecture. Price per share has a negative coefficient while the coefficient on firm size is positive; that is, low price apparently is the factor associated with higher realized returns. This result is consistent with an explanation of the size effect based on higher secondary market transaction costs for small firms. However, the fact that the coefficient of firm size becomes positive when price per share is included in the regression introduces a puzzle deserving further investigation.

Notes

1. Original recognition of the size effect is credited to Banz (1981). Reinganum (1981a, 1981b) also provides early empirical evidence of the size effect.

2. A perfect capital market implies that there are no impediments to frictionless and costless security transactions.

3. No attempt was made to exclude those firms whose fiscal year end was not 31 December. It is doubtful that the results of the study would change in a meaningful way if

such a restriction were imposed since over 62 percent of the firms have 31 December as fiscal year end.

4. These numbers are comparable to those reported by Reinganum (1981a, p. 35).

5. Where the number of stocks in a given year did not divide evenly into 10 portfolios, the smaller market value portfolios contain an additional stock.

6. Roll (1982) and Blume and Stambaugh (1983) derive related expressions.

7. This result supports the notion that low market value firms have high relative bid-ask spreads, something demonstrated by Stoll and Whaley (1983) and something to which we return later in this chapter.

8. Stocks with fewer than 5,000 shares traded during the year were ignored.

9. Lakonishok and Smidt (1984) analyze volume data at the turn of the year and show that a substantial fraction of the smallest companies had no transactions in a day.

10. Rogalski (1984) shows that the negative Monday return is due to the period between Friday close and Monday opening, not to the period between opening and close on Monday.

11. For a firm to be included in the sample in a particular year, it had to have continuous return data available for the entire year on the CRSP daily return file and financial statement data available for the year on the COMPUSTAT annual industrial file.

Appendix 6A: Tables

Table 6A–1
Summary of Empirical Evidence of the Size Effect

Study	Sample	Return Data	Risk Adjustment[a]	Average Annual Return Differential[b]
Banz (1981)	NYSE 1936–1975	Monthly	CAPM	12.12
Stoll and Whaley (1983)	NYSE 1960–1979	Monthly	CAPM	12.00
Reinganum (1981a)	NYSE/AMEX 1963–1975	Daily	None	21.16
Reinganum (1982)	NYSE/AMEX 1964–1978	Daily	CAPM	29.62
Keim (1983a)	NYSE/AMEX 1963–1979	Daily	CAPM	30.12
Blume and Stambaugh (1983)	NYSE/AMEX 1963–1980	Daily	None	26.36
Morgan et al. (1982)	Canadian 1963–1979	Monthly	CAPM	12.60
Brown et al. (1983)	Australian 1958–1981	Monthly	CAPM	63.36

[a]In the studies denoted by CAPM, the Sharpe (1964) and Lintner (1965) CAPM is used as a means of risk adjusting the portfolio returns. The studies denoted by None do not adjust portfolio returns for risk.

[b]The average annual return differential is defined as the difference between the mean realized returns of the smallest firm portfolio and the largest firm portfolio taken to an annual basis. There are assumed to be 251 trading days in a calendar year.

Table 6A–2
Number of Firms with Continuous Daily Returns on the CRSP File and with Financial Statement Data on the COMPUSTAT

Year	Number of Firms
1963	677
1964	718
1965	766
1966	815
1967	852
1968	919
1969	981
1970	1,087
1971	1,170
1972	1,247
1973	1,333
1974	1,369
1975	1,395
1976	1,414
1977	1,448
1978	1,480
1979	1,509
1980	1,538
1981	1,597
Total	22,315

Table 6A–3
Average Annual Rates of Return for Ten Portfolios Arranged in Ascending Order of Size

Portfolio Number	Average Market Value[a]	Average Annual Return (Geometric)[b]	Average Annual Return (Arithmetic)[c]
1	4.6	.50277	.35176
2	11.2	.33364	.24602
3	20.9	.27310	.20726
4	35.1	.22542	.17221
5	58.3	.19647	.15728
6	99.1	.18398	.15036
7	172.7	.15381	.12821
8	319.3	.14646	.12507
9	618.1	.11906	.10362
10	2,989.5	.08963	.08145

Note: Table values are arithmetic averages of the average market value and the portfolio rates of return for the 19 years 1963 through 1981.

[a]Average market value of common stock is the 19-year average of the mean common stock value within the portfolio in a given year and is expressed in millions of dollars.

[b]The annual portfolio rate of return with geometric compounding is

$$\bar{R}_p = \prod_{t=1}^{T} (1 + R_{pt}) - 1,$$

where R_{pt} is the portfolio return in trading day t and T is the number of trading days in the year.

[c]The annual portfolio rate of return with arithmetic compounding is

$$\bar{R}_p = \sum_{t=1}^{T} R_{pt} .$$

Table 6A–4
Sample Stocks by Stock Exchange for the Ten Portfolios Arranged in Ascending Order of Size

Portfolio Number	Average Market Value[a]	Proportion of Portfolio's Stocks		
		NYSE	AMEX	OTC and Regional
1	4.6	.073	.861	.066
2	11.2	.300	.659	.041
3	20.9	.541	.423	.036
4	35.1	.720	.260	.020
5	58.3	.846	.135	.019
6	99.1	.899	.085	.016
7	172.7	.920	.066	.014
8	319.3	.944	.048	.010
9	618.1	.974	.024	.002
10	2,989.5	.976	.024	.000

[a]Average market value of common stock is the 19-year average of the mean common stock value within the portfolio in a given year and is expressed in millions of dollars.

Table 6A–5
Average Variance and First-Order Serial Covariance Estimates for Ten Portfolios Arranged in Ascending Order of Size

Portfolio Number	Average Market Value[a]	Arithmetic Average Annual Return, $\bar{R}_{AR}$	Average Cross-Sectional Variance, σ_μ^2	Average Stock Serial Covariance, $\bar{\sigma}_{\varepsilon_1, \varepsilon_2}$	Average Portfolio Serial Covariance, $\bar{\sigma}_{\varepsilon_1, \varepsilon_2}$	Average Total Bias, $\bar{\sigma}_{\varepsilon_1, \varepsilon_2} - \bar{\sigma}_{\varepsilon_1, \varepsilon_2} - \sigma_\mu^2$
1	4.6	.35176	.00081	−.06392	.00846	.07157
2	11.2	.24602	.00065	−.03155	.00683	.03772
3	20.9	.20726	.00056	−.01458	.00679	.02081
4	35.1	.17221	.00051	−.00547	.00686	.01183
5	58.3	.15728	.00046	.00055	.00643	.00542
6	99.1	.15036	.00040	.00182	.00542	.00320
7	172.7	.12821	.00035	.00370	.00531	.00126
8	319.3	.12507	.00030	.00450	.00485	.00006
9	618.1	.10362	.00023	.00484	.00432	−.00074
10	2,989.5	.08145	.00019	.00474	.00371	−.00122

Note: Table values are arithmetic averages of parameter estimates obtained for each of the years 1963 through 1981.
[a] Average market value of common stock is expressed in millions of dollars.

Table 6A–6
Average Annual Rebalanced and Buy-and-Hold Rates of Return for Ten Portfolios Arranged in Ascending Order of Size

Portfolio Number	Average Market Value[a]	Average Annual Portfolio Return by Compounding Interval						Rebalanced (Daily) Less Buy-and-Hold (Annual)
		Annual	Semiannual	Quarterly	Monthly	Weekly	Daily	
1	4.6	.29670	.30217	.30203	.32682	.39971	.50277	.20608
2	11.2	.24746	.23872	.23733	.24694	.28291	.33364	.08618
3	20.9	.22468	.21744	.21475	.21941	.24436	.27310	.04841
4	35.1	.19203	.18560	.18303	.18735	.20650	.22542	.03339
5	58.3	.17903	.17293	.16739	.17047	.18493	.19647	.01744
6	99.1	.17124	.16614	.16286	.16439	.17567	.18398	.01274
7	172.7	.14312	.14061	.13692	.13943	.14809	.15381	.01069
8	319.3	.14041	.13683	.13441	.13668	.14341	.14646	.00605
9	618.1	.11225	.11167	.10899	.11196	.11722	.11906	.00680
10	2,989.5	.08710	.08560	.08381	.08592	.08909	.08963	.00252

Note: Table values are arithmetic averages of the portfolio returns for each of the years 1963 through 1981.
[a]Average market value of common stock is expressed in millions of dollars.

Table 6A–7
Average Holding Period Length in Years for Stocks in Ten Portfolios Arranged
in Ascending Order of Size

| Portfolio Number | Average Market Value[a] | *Holding Period Estimates (Years)* | | |
		Stocks[b] (shares)	Portfolio[c] (shares)	Portfolio[d] Values
1	4.6	6.403	3.963	3.792
2	11.2	6.122	3.400	3.296
3	20.9	5.359	2.931	2.955
4	35.1	5.051	2.685	2.706
5	58.3	5.191	2.673	2.709
6	99.1	6.739	3.045	3.083
7	172.7	10.305	3.367	3.327
8	319.3	44.387	4.165	3.904
9	618.1	83.656	5.867	4.925
10	2,989.5	112.727	8.831	8.511

Note: Table values are arithmetic averages of the values obtained in each of the years 1963 through 1981.

[a]Average market value of common stock is expressed in millions of dollars.

[b]Average holding period length for the portfolio in a given year is computed as

$$\frac{1}{n} \sum_{j=1}^{n} \frac{\text{number of shares outstanding}_j}{\text{number of shares traded}_j},$$

where n is the number of stocks in the portfolio.

[c]Average holding period length for the portfolio in a given year is computed as

$$\frac{\sum_{j=1}^{n} \text{number of shares outstanding}_j}{\sum_{j=1}^{n} \text{number of shares traded}_j}.$$

[d]Average holding period length for the portfolio in a given year is computed as

$$\frac{\sum_{j=1}^{n} \text{number of shares outstanding}_j \times \text{price per share}_j}{\sum_{j=1}^{n} \text{number of shares traded}_j \times \text{price per share}_j}.$$

Table 6A–8
Average 3-Year Rebalanced, Arithmetic, and Buy-and-Hold Rates of Return for Ten Portfolios Arranged in Ascending Order of Size

Portfolio Number	Average Market Value[a]	Average 3-Year Portfolio Return		
		Rebalanced[b]	Arithmetic[c]	Buy-and-Hold[d]
1	4.5	2.37780	1.05058	2.13340
2	11.0	1.47080	.78131	2.01948
3	20.2	1.08116	.63795	1.84040
4	33.7	.81695	.52055	1.67698
5	56.0	.72718	.48726	1.62432
6	94.9	.64613	.45484	1.58800
7	165.5	.51489	.37903	1.47626
8	306.9	.43639	.33922	1.40825
9	594.4	.36328	.29950	1.33928
10	2,925.8	.25119	.23033	1.24082

Note: Table values are arithmetic averages of the portfolio returns for each of the years 1963 through 1979.

[a]Average market value is expressed in millions of dollars.

[b]Rebalanced portfolio return is computed as

$$\prod_{t=1}^{T} \left(1 + \frac{1}{n} \sum_{j=1}^{n} R_{jt} \right) - 1,$$

where T is the number of trading days in the 3-year period.

[c]Arithmetic portfolio return is computed as

$$\sum_{t=1}^{T} \frac{1}{n} \sum_{j=1}^{n} R_{jt}.$$

[d]Buy-and-hold portfolio return is computed as

$$\frac{1}{n} \sum_{j=1}^{n} \left[\prod_{t=1}^{T} (1 + R_{jt}) - 1 \right].$$

Table 6A–9
Number of Zero Daily Returns Observations, Total Number of Daily Return Observations, and Zero Daily Return Observations as a Proportion of Total for Stocks in Ten Portfolios Arranged in Ascending Order of Size during the 19-Year Period, 1963–1981

Portfolio Number	Average Market Value[a]	Number of Zero Returns	Total Number of Returns	Proportion of Zero Returns
1	4.6	195,640	562,398	.3479
2	11.2	164,659	562,148	.2929
3	20.9	141,861	561,897	.2525
4	35.1	123,831	561,645	.2205
5	58.3	110,502	561,392	.1968
6	99.1	101,597	560,887	.1815
7	172.7	94,158	560,835	.1679
8	319.3	86,706	559,626	.1549
9	618.1	81,020	558,868	.1450
10	2,989.5	66,419	558,136	.1190

[a]Average market value of common stock is expressed in millions of dollars.

Table 6A–10
Average Daily Rates of Return, by Day of Week, for Ten Portfolios Arranged in Ascending Order of Size

Portfolio Number	Average Market Value[a]	Average Daily Rates of Return (Annualized)					Equal-Weighted Average	Overall Average
		Monday	Tuesday	Wednesday	Thursday	Friday		
1	4.6	−.01434	.01502	.47907	.42082	.86748	.35361	.36176
2	11.2	−.27154	−.01530	.41161	.36458	.74655	.24718	.24602
3	20.9	−.33521	−.04689	.38005	.29854	.74065	.20743	.20726
4	35.1	−.37507	−.04144	.37017	.26507	.64065	.17187	.17221
5	58.3	−.34336	−.02226	.35718	.23697	.55995	.15770	.15728
6	99.1	−.36067	.02055	.34465	.23558	.51044	.15011	.15036
7	172.7	−.35119	−.00917	.33975	.20738	.45315	.12798	.12821
8	319.3	−.32576	.03911	.33603	.20367	.36404	.12342	.12507
9	618.1	−.29612	.03221	.29516	.15587	.32854	.10313	.10362
10	2,989.5	−.32334	.08871	.27527	.12366	.23680	.08022	.08145

Note: Table values are arithmetic averages of the parameter estimates obtained for each of the years 1963 through 1981.
[a]Average market value of common stock is expressed in millions of dollars.

Table 6A–11
Average Portfolio Systematic Risk Estimates for Ten Portfolios Arranged in Ascending Order of Size

Portfolio Number	Average Market Value[a]	OLS Regression $(\hat{\beta}_p)$	ACM:[b] One Leading, One Lagged $(\hat{\beta}_p)$	ACM:[b] Two Leading, Two Lagged $(\hat{\beta}_p)$
1	4.6	.98922	1.26890	1.51244
2	11.2	1.02265	1.28792	1.44734
3	20.9	1.10656	1.30167	1.43837
4	35.1	1.14169	1.31767	1.44565
5	58.3	1.14753	1.31555	1.44183
6	99.1	1.06198	1.21565	1.29306
7	172.7	1.05897	1.19133	1.26747
8	319.3	1.02823	1.12810	1.20094
9	618.1	.98564	1.06140	1.09608
10	2,989.5	.99893	.99995	.99967

Note: Table values are arithmetic averages of the parameter estimates obtained for each of the years 1963 through 1981.

[a]Average market value is expressed in millions of dollars.

[b]ACM = Aggregated coefficients model.

Table 6A–12
Average Raw and Risk-Adjusted Rates of Return for Ten Portfolios Arranged in Ascending Order of Size

Portfolio Number	Total Market Value[a]	Average Annual Return	Average Annual Return (Excluding January)	Systematic Risk	Average Risk-Adjusted Return
1	4.6	.29670	.13487	1.51244	.19513
2	11.2	.24746	.12946	1.44734	.10818
3	20.9	.22468	.13083	1.43837	.08582
4	35.1	.19203	.10805	1.44565	.07153
5	58.3	.17903	.11160	1.44183	.06493
6	99.1	.17124	.12047	1.29306	.06647
7	172.7	.14312	.09753	1.26747	.04984
8	319.3	.14041	.10951	1.20094	.05631
9	618.1	.11225	.09028	1.09608	.03736
10	2,989.5	.08710	.07898	.99967	.00853

Note: Table values are arithmetic averages of parameter estimates obtained for each of the years 1963 through 1981.

[a]Average market value is expressed in millions of dollars.

Table 6A–13
Summary of Cross-Sectional Regression Results of the Ex Post Sharpe-Lintner Model

$$R_j - R_f = \hat{\gamma}_0 + \hat{\gamma}_1 \beta_j$$

Year	Number of Observations	$\hat{\gamma}_0$	$t(\hat{\gamma}_0)$	$\hat{\gamma}_1$	$t(\hat{\gamma}_1)$	$\bar{R}^2$
1963	677	.09963	6.65	.05193	5.12	.03603
1964	718	.13131	8.19	.02610	2.57	.00777
1965	766	.00387	.12	.25056	12.41	.16675
1966	815	− .22997	− 11.99	.10919	7.64	.06591
1967	852	.53206	8.97	.14691	4.02	.01746
1968	919	.31883	8.41	.00815	.32	− .00098
1969	981	− .17294	− 8.60	− .07413	− 5.57	.02967
1970	1,087	.07785	3.87	− .17975	− 13.00	.13395
1971	1,170	.11468	4.55	.03781	2.48	.00439
1972	1,247	.05134	3.11	− .00208	− .25	− .00075
1973	1,333	− .13084	− 7.60	− .12914	− 15.26	.14824
1974	1,369	− .36440	− 26.49	.02998	5.71	.02257
1975	1,395	.25818	8.48	.22062	11.53	.08647
1976	1,414	.27021	14.37	.06545	7.79	.04052
1977	1,448	.08125	6.57	− .00603	− .57	− .00047
1978	1,480	− .08510	− 4.32	.12786	10.62	.07033
1979	1,509	.10749	3.62	.14161	7.43	.03472
1980	1,538	.00998	.38	.17500	9.15	.05106
1981	1,597	− .14642	− 10.06	.03839	4.55	.01219
$\bar{\gamma}_i$		.04879		.05465		.04873
$t(\bar{\gamma}_i)$		1.00		2.15		
$p[t(\bar{\gamma}_i)]$		.328		.045		

Note: R_j denotes the annual realized rate of return on stock j; R_f, the riskless rate of return; and β_j, the estimated systematic risk coefficient of stock j.

Table 6A–14
Rates of Return on Standard & Poor's 500 Index, CRSP Value-Weighted
Market Index, CRSP Equal-Weighted Market Index, and One-Year U.S.
Treasury Bills

	Market Returns (R_m)			
Year	Standard & Poor's	Value Weighted	Equal Weighted	R_f
1963	.18881	.20988	.21589	.02940
1964	.12961	.16245	.23586	.03660
1965	.09060	.14283	.40374	.03930
1966	−.13089	−.08766	−.02967	.04700
1967	.20091	.28611	.81338	.04900
1968	.07660	.14446	.44175	.05500
1969	−.11359	−.10815	−.23714	.06240
1970	.00103	.00163	−.06677	.07750
1971	.10788	.15928	.24444	.04860
1972	.15642	.17347	.08423	.04090
1973	−.17368	−.17877	−.30600	.05440
1974	−.29716	−.27222	−.18135	.06940
1975	.31562	.37469	.80551	.06700
1976	.19144	.26441	.57861	.05770
1977	−.11501	−.04126	.19335	.04760
1978	.01063	.07679	.23206	.06570
1979	.12302	.23527	.43888	.09610
1980	.25774	.32692	.38678	.10970
1981	−.09731	−.04472	.08455	.12380
Mean	.04856	.09607	.22832	.06195

Table 6A–15

Summary of Cross-Sectional Regression Results of the Ex Post Sharpe-Lintner Model with Firm Size Included as an Additional Explanatory Variable

$R_j - R_f = \hat{\gamma}_0 + \hat{\gamma}_1 \beta_j + \hat{\gamma}_2 S_j$

Year	Number of Observations	$\hat{\gamma}_0$	$t(\hat{\gamma}_0)$	$\hat{\gamma}_1$	$t(\hat{\gamma}_1)$	$\hat{\gamma}_2$	$t(\hat{\gamma}_2)$	$\bar{R}^2$
1963	677	.09722	6.40	.05170	5.10	.00752	.94	.03587
1964	718	.13291	8.18	.02614	2.58	−.00406	−.60	.00688
1965	766	.01537	0.45	.24766	12.24	−.01738	−1.71	.16885
1966	815	−.22919	−11.77	.10902	7.62	−.00127	−.24	.06482
1967	852	.57410	9.51	.13718	3.76	−.07304	−3.28	.02864
1968	919	.34462	8.94	.00074	.03	−.03462	−3.23	.00922
1969	981	−.18675	9.02	−.06904	−5.15	.01383	2.68	.03575
1970	1,087	.07418	3.62	−.17842	−12.83	−.00460	.90	.13381
1971	1,170	.11848	4.58	.03651	2.37	−.00480	.65	.00389
1972	1,247	.04232	2.50	−.00027	−.03	.01449	2.30	.00270
1973	1,333	−.13614	−7.61	−.12742	−14.81	.14460	1.10	.14837
1974	1,369	−.36381	−25.75	.02990	5.67	−.00122	−.18	.02188
1975	1,395	.27001	8.73	.21758	11.35	.02092	−2.08	.08865
1976	1,414	.28404	14.71	.06223	7.37	.02222	−3.02	.04601
1977	1,448	.08948	7.20	−.00486	−.46	−.02071	−4.35	.01177
1978	1,480	−.08290	−4.10	.12716	10.49	−.00301	−.50	.06985
1979	1,509	.11928	3.92	.13745	7.16	−.01483	−1.76	.03607
1980	1,538	.00533	.20	.17649	9.18	−.00588	.78	.05081
1981	1,597	−.13714	9.11	.03634	4.29	−.01059	−2.37	.01505
$\bar{\gamma}_i$		.05428		.05348		−.00978		.05152
$t(\bar{\gamma}_i)$		1.07		2.13		−2.06		
$p[t(\bar{\gamma}_i)]$		.298		.046		.053		

Note: R_j denotes the annual realized rate of return on stock j; R_f, the riskless rate of interest; β_j, the estimated systematic risk coefficient of stock j; and S_j, the total market value of firm j's common stock.

Table 6A–16
Summary of Cross-Sectional Regression Results of the Ex Post Brennan Model

$$R_i - R_f = \hat{\gamma}_0 + \hat{\gamma}_1\beta_i + \hat{\gamma}_2\,(d_i - R_f)$$

Year	Number of Observations	$\hat{\gamma}_0$	$t(\hat{\gamma}_0)$	$\hat{\gamma}_1$	$t(\hat{\gamma}_1)$	$\hat{\gamma}_2$	$t(\hat{\gamma}_2)$	$\bar{R}^2$
1963	677	.09748	6.63	.04550	4.55	2.89977	5.31	.07340
1964	718	.13900	8.67	.02992	2.96	2.11186	3.57	.02377
1965	766	− .00438	.13	.25139	12.15	.18104	.18	.16570
1966	815	− .21838	−11.17	.12401	8.16	1.51608	2.76	.07347
1967	852	.41526	6.99	.11947	3.36	−10.61679	7.71	.08067
1968	919	.31574	8.10	.00371	.13	− .30574	.34	− .00195
1969	981	− .13719	− 5.41	− .05783	− 3.84	1.39695	2.30	.03393
1970	1,087	.23206	10.93	.08911	6.32	5.39349	14.55	.27483
1971	1,170	.11187	4.43	.02471	1.43	.95146	− 1.62	.00577
1972	1,247	.06325	3.70	.00364	.42	1.19977	2.56	.00368
1973	1,333	− .11675	− 6.75	− .11062	−12.10	1.60086	5.09	.16388
1974	1,369	− .29721	−19.49	.03242	6.35	2.54183	9.14	.07828
1975	1,395	.23269	7.64	.25358	12.79	1.85510	5.57	.10578
1976	1,414	.27129	14.55	.07871	9.01	1.70839	5.07	.05701
1977	1,448	.08346	6.69	− .00420	.39	.39369	1.26	− .00005
1978	1,480	− .08541	− 4.32	.12702	10.07	− .06631	.22	.06973
1979	1,509	.09139	2.94	.13244	6.72	− .60739	− 1.79	.03613
1980	1,538	− .02328	.79	.15533	7.52	.87111	2.51	.05431
1981	1,597	− .06717	− 3.83	.04706	5.63	1.11674	7.80	.04792
$\bar{\gamma}_i$		.05855		.06143		.55246		.07086
$t(\bar{\gamma}_i)$		1.36		2.68		.78		
$p[t(\bar{\gamma}_i)]$		.188		.015		.448		

Note: R_i denotes the annual realized rate of return on stock i; R_f, the riskless rate of interest; β_i, the estimated systematic risk coefficient of stock i; and d_i, the dividend yield of stock i.

Table 6A–17
Summary of Simple Correlation Coefficient Estimates between Total Firm Size and Dividend Yield

Year	Number of Observations	Correlation Coefficient, $\hat{r}$	$t(\hat{r})$
1963	677	.05196	1.35
1964	718	.02814	.75
1965	766	.02913	.81
1966	815	.04389	1.25
1967	852	.01493	.44
1968	919	.04012	1.22
1969	981	.11418	3.60
1970	1,087	.05310	1.75
1971	1,170	.07664	2.63
1972	1,247	.06659	2.35
1973	1,333	.02566	.94
1974	1,369	−.01817	− .67
1975	1,395	.00186	.07
1976	1,414	.02964	1.11
1977	1,448	.06205	2.36
1978	1,480	.07779	3.00
1979	1,509	.06812	2.65
1980	1,538	.09390	3.70
1981	1,597	.03403	1.36
Mean		.04894	

Table 6A–18
Summary of Cross-Sectional Regression Results of the Ex Post Brennan Model with Firm Size Included as an Additional Explanatory Variable

$$R_j - R_f = \hat{\gamma}_0 + \hat{\gamma}_1 \beta_j + \hat{\gamma}_2(d_j - R_f) + \hat{\gamma}_3 S_j$$

Year	Number of Observations	$\hat{\gamma}_0$	$t(\hat{\gamma}_0)$	$\hat{\gamma}_1$	$t(\hat{\gamma}_1)$	$\hat{\gamma}_2$	$t(\hat{\gamma}_2)$	$\hat{\gamma}_3$	$t(\hat{\gamma}_3)$	$\bar{R}^2$
1963	677	.09573	6.42	.04537	4.53	2.88090	5.27	.00548	.70	.07269
1964	718	.14092	8.66	.02999	2.96	2.12402	3.59	.00477	.71	.02308
1965	766	.01594	.47	.24857	11.99	.20001	.20	−.01740	−1.71	.16781
1966	815	−.21731	−10.94	.12384	8.14	1.52098	2.77	−.00168	−.32	.07244
1967	852	.45698	7.58	.10997	3.10	−10.58543	−7.73	−.07190	−3.34	.09155
1968	919	.34152	8.62	−.00372	−.13	−.30694	−.34	−.03462	−3.23	.00826
1969	981	−.15256	−5.87	−.05394	−3.57	1.31261	2.17	.01322	2.56	.03939
1970	1,087	.22872	10.61	−.08798	−6.21	5.39106	14.54	.00409	.88	.27467
1971	1,170	.11552	4.45	.02355	1.36	.94518	1.61	−.00459	.62	.00524
1972	1,247	.05420	3.09	.00515	.59	1.15409	2.46	.01381	2.20	.00673
1973	1,333	−.12313	−6.88	.10823	−11.63	1.62327	5.15	.00572	1.37	.16443
1974	1,369	−.29725	−19.13	.03242	6.63	2.54192	9.14	.00010	.02	.07761
1975	1,395	.24403	7.88	.25046	12.60	1.84067	5.54	.02735	−1.98	.10766
1976	1,414	.28492	14.89	.07547	8.60	1.69965	5.06	.02190	−3.00	.06234
1977	1,448	.09239	7.35	−.00258	−.24	.48484	1.56	.02120	−4.44	.01276
1978	1,480	−.08323	−4.11	.12641	9.97	.05982	.20	−.00296	−.49	.06925
1979	1,509	.10332	3.25	.12876	6.50	−.58562	−1.73	.01428	−1.70	.03734
1980	1,538	−.02961	−.98	.15668	7.57	−.89089	−2.56	.00705	.93	.05423
1981	1,597	−.05672	−3.16	.04492	5.36	1.12439	7.87	−.01131	−2.58	.05129
$\bar{\gamma}_i$		.06391		.06027		.55397		−.00971		.07362
$t(\bar{\gamma}_i)$		1.42		2.67		.78		−2.08		
$p[t(\bar{\gamma}_i)]$		.171		.015		.445		.051		

Note: R_j denotes the annual realized rate of return on stock j; R_f, the riskless rate of interest; β_j, the estimated systematic risk coefficient of stock j; d_j, the dividend yield of stock j; and S_j, the total market value of firm j's common stock.

Table 6A–19
Summary of Cross-Sectional Regression Results of the Ex Post Sharpe-Lintner Model with Earnings Yield Included as an Additional Explanatory Variable

$$R_i - R_f = \hat{\gamma}_0 + \hat{\gamma}_1\beta_i + \hat{\gamma}_2 e_i$$

Year	Number of Observations	$\hat{\gamma}_0$	$t(\hat{\gamma}_0)$	$\hat{\gamma}_1$	$t(\hat{\gamma}_1)$	$\hat{\gamma}_2$	$t(\hat{\gamma}_2)$	$\bar{R}^2$
1963	677	.03658	2.38	.02472	2.51	1.36616	10.01	.15963
1964	718	.02186	1.23	.02588	2.76	1.48369	11.02	.15066
1965	766	−.15720	−4.58	.23134	12.29	2.27976	11.07	.28116
1966	815	−.32413	−15.12	.10161	7.41	1.31351	8.54	.14179
1967	852	.19826	3.01	.10113	2.89	4.37332	9.76	.11561
1968	919	.13628	3.07	.03293	1.31	2.37015	7.39	.05430
1969	981	−.36677	−14.41	−.03468	−2.67	2.98331	11.37	.14213
1970	1,087	−.05821	−3.01	−.14539	−11.77	1.85046	17.60	.32587
1971	1,170	.02286	.86	.06745	4.60	1.64866	11.58	.10628
1972	1,247	−.06962	−3.69	−.00309	−.38	1.84306	11.51	.09476
1973	1,333	−.24587	−13.17	−.12321	−15.37	1.25336	12.58	.23827
1974	1,369	−.44985	−34.29	.02924	6.23	.72135	18.61	.21971
1975	1,395	.21842	7.28	.23368	12.50	.20033	8.76	.13362
1976	1,414	.22663	12.10	.07160	8.78	.27216	9.84	.10149
1977	1,448	.01910	1.48	−.01094	−1.09	.55498	12.03	.08994
1978	1,480	−.14211	−7.22	.11795	10.15	.51039	10.86	.13851
1979	1,509	−.04700	−1.58	.14366	8.07	.94402	14.84	.15732
1980	1,538	−.06814	−2.55	.18576	9.99	.58579	9.88	.10716
1981	1,597	−.22189	−16.43	.03472	4.61	.86133	20.30	.21457
$\bar{\gamma}_i$		−.06929		.05707		1.44294		.15646
$t(\bar{\gamma}_i)$		−1.55		2.44		6.06		
$p[\|t(\bar{\gamma}_i)\|]$		.137		.025		.000		

Note: R_i denotes the annual realized rate of return on stock i; R_f, the riskless rate of interest; β_i, the estimated systematic risk coefficient of stock i; and e_i, the earnings yield of stock i.

Table 6A–20
Summary of Simple Correlation Coefficient Estimates between Firm Size and Earnings Yield

Year	Number of Observations	Correlation Coefficient, $\hat{r}$	$t(\hat{r})$
1963	677	.00371	.10
1964	718	−.02951	− .79
1965	766	−.04634	−1.28
1966	815	−.06581	−1.88
1967	852	−.07724	−2.26
1968	919	−.02002	− .61
1969	981	.05181	1.62
1970	1,087	.01872	.62
1971	1,170	.01764	.60
1972	1,247	−.00705	− .25
1973	1,333	−.03951	−1.44
1974	1,369	−.02016	− .75
1975	1,395	.00602	.22
1976	1,414	−.00135	− .05
1977	1,448	−.01094	− .42
1978	1,480	−.00120	− .05
1979	1,509	.00823	.32
1980	1,538	.03974	1.56
1981	1,597	.03128	1.25
Mean		.02612	

Table 6A–21
Summary of Cross-Sectional Regression Results of the Sharpe-Lintner Model with Earnings Yield and Firm Size Included as Additional Explanatory Variable

$$R_j - R_f = \hat{\gamma}_0 + \hat{\gamma}_1\beta_j + \hat{\gamma}_2 e_j + \hat{\gamma}_3 S_j$$

Year	Number of Observations	$\hat{\gamma}_0$	$t(\hat{\gamma}_0)$	$\hat{\gamma}_1$	$t(\hat{\gamma}_1)$	$\hat{\gamma}_2$	$t(\hat{\gamma}_2)$	$\hat{\gamma}_3$	$t(\hat{\gamma}_3)$	$\bar{R}^2$
1963	677	.03407	2.19	.02447	2.49	1.36661	10.02	.00776	1.04	.15974
1964	718	.02275	1.26	.02591	2.76	1.48242	11.00	−.00201	−.32	.14959
1965	766	−.14758	−4.22	.22921	12.14	2.26845	11.02	−.01333	−1.41	.28209
1966	815	−.32524	−14.93	.10179	7.41	1.31631	8.53	.00149	.29	.14082
1967	852	.23886	3.56	.09410	2.69	4.28913	9.59	−.05938	−2.80	.12269
1968	919	.16268	3.62	.02571	1.02	2.33827	7.32	−.03215	−3.08	.06300
1969	981	−.37911	−14.70	−.03001	−2.30	2.97306	11.37	.01302	2.68	.14753
1970	1,087	−.06173	−3.14	−.14412	−11.60	1.85024	17.60	−.00443	.99	.32585
1971	1,170	.01937	.71	.06626	4.48	1.64818	11.58	−.00436	.62	.10580
1972	1,247	−.07907	−4.11	−.00122	−.15	1.84548	11.54	.01491	2.49	.09854
1973	1,333	−.25497	−13.19	−.12049	−14.78	1.26256	12.67	.00718	1.81	.23956
1974	1,369	−.45031	−33.47	.02930	6.22	.72147	18.60	.00093	.16	.21915
1975	1,395	.23024	7.56	.23065	12.32	.20032	8.77	−.02902	−2.14	.13583
1976	1,414	.24012	12.50	.06847	8.35	.27123	9.83	−.02144	−3.01	.10660
1977	1,448	.02733	2.11	−.00979	.98	.55255	12.05	−.02005	−4.42	.10144
1978	1,480	−.13957	−6.93	.11712	10.01	.51062	10.86	−.00353	−.60	.13814
1979	1,509	−.03468	−1.15	.13926	7.77	.94495	14.87	−.01568	−2.00	.15899
1980	1,538	−.07071	−2.59	.18660	9.99	.58485	9.85	.00341	.47	.10671
1981	1,597	−.21061	−15.18	.03211	4.26	.86615	20.46	−.01336	−3.36	.21960
$\bar{\gamma}_j$		−.06405		.05607		1.43647		−.00848		.15904
$t(\bar{\gamma}_j)$		−1.38		2.43		6.13		−2.01		
$p[|t(\bar{\gamma}_j)|]$		.184		.025		.000		.058		

Note: R_j denotes the annual realized rate of return of stock j; R_f, the riskless rate of interest; β, the estimated systematic risk coefficient; e_j, the earnings yield of stock j; and S_j, the total market value of firm j's common stock.

Table 6A–22
Summary of Cross-Sectional Regression Results of Systematic Risk as a Function of Debt-Equity Ratio

$$\beta_j = \hat{\gamma}_0 + \hat{\gamma}_1 D_j$$

Year	Number of Observations	$\hat{\gamma}_1$	$t(\hat{\gamma}_0)$	$\hat{\gamma}_1$	$t(\hat{\gamma}_1)$	$\bar{R}^2$
1963	677	.92413	17.56	−.04595	− .62	−.00091
1964	718	.98225	18.12	.04707	.60	−.00089
1965	766	1.30715	31.55	.09464	1.66	.00229
1966	815	1.18192	40.49	−.11020	−2.46	.00618
1967	852	1.23327	30.97	.14211	3.05	.00963
1968	919	1.34348	43.21	−.25205	−5.22	.02783
1969	981	1.37010	45.66	−.14477	−2.33	.00448
1970	1,087	1.32897	51.74	−.06494	−1.88	.00233
1971	1,170	1.42860	50.14	.01955	.71	−.00042
1972	1,247	1.42334	30.99	.07082	1.41	.00079
1973	1,333	1.81374	55.77	−.06411	−2.25	.00303
1974	1,369	1.62274	23.86	−.03373	−1.05	.00008
1975	1,395	1.26328	47.80	.03841	5.54	.02086
1976	1,414	1.65698	39.91	.08797	5.50	.02027
1977	1,448	.81387	31.30	−.01268	− .92	−.00010
1978	1,480	1.34062	52.14	.05022	3.95	.00977
1979	1,509	1.30607	54.64	.04366	3.43	.00710
1980	1,538	1.22199	60.21	−.03563	−3.18	.00591
1981	1,597	1.33094	43.36	−.02387	−1.61	.00101
$\bar{\gamma}_i$		1.31018		−.01018		.00628
$t(\bar{\gamma}_i)$		23.76		− .47		
$p[t(\bar{\gamma}_i)]$		.000		.642		

Note: β_j denotes the estimated systematic risk of stock j; D_j, denotes firm j's long-term debt to market value of common stock ratio.

Table 6A-23
Summary of Cross-Sectional Regression Results of the Ex Post Sharpe-Lintner Model with Debt-Equity Ratio Included as an Additional Explanatory Variable

$$R_i - R_f = \hat{\gamma}_0 + \hat{\gamma}_1\beta_i + \hat{\gamma}_2 D_i$$

Year	Number of Observations	$\hat{\gamma}_0$	$t(\hat{\gamma}_0)$	$\hat{\gamma}_1$	$t(\hat{\gamma}_1)$	$\hat{\gamma}_2$	$t(\hat{\gamma}_2)$	$\bar{R}^2$
1963	677	.08260	4.95	.05248	5.19	.04458	2.30	.04209
1964	718	.10757	6.09	−.02540	2.52	.06560	3.10	.01954
1965	766	−.03275	−.94	.24640	12.27	.10963	3.46	.17854
1966	815	−.22661	−10.93	.10866	7.58	.00785	−1.43	.06497
1967	852	.49958	8.03	.14036	3.82	.08620	1.72	.01970
1968	919	.28077	6.58	.01671	.64	.07460	−1.94	.00201
1969	981	−.14631	−6.62	−.07694	−5.78	.07404	−2.85	.03667
1970	1,087	.03702	1.71	−.17595	−12.84	.07594	4.86	.15163
1971	1,170	.12537	4.76	.03825	2.51	.01985	−1.39	.00517
1972	1,247	.07237	3.99	−.00116	.14	.04090	−2.74	.00446
1973	1,333	−.12285	−6.69	−.12978	−15.31	.01100	−1.24	.14859
1974	1,369	−.37370	−23.78	.03016	5.74	.00762	1.22	.02292
1975	1,395	.26242	8.46	.22267	11.51	.00366	−.72	.08616
1976	1,414	.25421	13.21	.06104	7.22	.01854	3.61	.04862
1977	1,448	.06726	4.98	−.00537	.51	.01408	2.56	.00336
1978	1,480	−.10527	−5.26	.12198	10.16	.02829	4.79	.08394
1979	1,509	.09902	3.23	.13969	7.30	.01077	1.14	.03491
1980	1,538	.04142	1.49	.16987	8.88	−.02792	−3.32	.05719
1981	1,597	−.15300	−10.01	.03888	4.60	.00707	1.42	.01281
$\bar{\gamma}_j$		.04048		.05386		.01883		.05386
$t(\bar{\gamma}_j)$		.86		2.15		1.73		
$p[t(\bar{\gamma}_j)]$		.398		.045		.100		

Note: R_i denotes the annual realized rate of return of stock i; R_f, the riskless rate of interest; β_i, the estimated systematic risk of stock i; and D_i, firm i's long-term debt to market value of common stock ratio.

Table 6A–24
Summary of Simple Correlation Coefficient Estimates between Firm Size and Ratio of Debt to Equity

Year	Number of Observations	Correlation Coefficient, $\hat{r}$	$t(\hat{r})$
1963	677	−.05473	−1.42
1964	718	−.06462	−1.73
1965	766	−.06834	−1.89
1966	815	−.06397	−1.83
1967	852	−.07206	−2.11
1968	919	−.05616	−1.70
1969	981	−.04379	−1.37
1970	1,087	−.06335	−2.09
1971	1,170	−.05080	−1.74
1972	1,247	−.06358	−2.25
1973	1,333	−.07123	−2.61
1974	1,369	−.09395	−3.49
1975	1,395	−.08008	−3.00
1976	1,414	−.07364	−2.77
1977	1,448	−.06453	−2.46
1978	1,480	−.05245	−2.02
1979	1,509	−.05657	−2.20
1980	1,538	−.05417	−2.13
1981	1,597	−.05075	−2.03
Mean		−.06309	

Table 6A–25
Summary of Cross-Sectional Regression Results of the Ex Post Sharpe-Lintner Model with Debt-Equity Ratio and Firm Size Included as Additional Explanatory Variables

$$R_j - R_f = \hat{\gamma}_0 + \hat{\gamma}_1 \beta_j + \hat{\gamma}_2 D_j + \hat{\gamma}_3 S_j$$

Year	Number of Observations	$\hat{\gamma}_0$	$t(\hat{\gamma}_0)$	$\hat{\gamma}_1$	$t(\hat{\gamma}_1)$	$\hat{\gamma}_2$	$t(\hat{\gamma}_2)$	$\hat{\gamma}_3$	$t(\hat{\gamma}_3)$	$\bar{R}^2$
1963	677	.07943	4.69	.05223	5.17	.04571	2.35	.00854	1.07	.04230
1964	718	.10884	6.06	.02543	2.52	.06505	3.06	−.00271	−.40	.01839
1965	766	−.02167	.61	.24398	12.12	.10658	3.36	−.01522	−1.51	.17990
1966	815	−.22559	−10.69	.10845	7.54	−.00819	−.44	−.00143	−.27	.06390
1967	852	.54422	8.57	.13169	3.59	.07597	1.52	−.07087	−3.18	.03013
1968	919	.30999	7.13	.00858	.33	.06593	1.71	−.03328	−3.10	.01131
1969	981	−.16066	−7.06	−.07199	−5.37	−.07042	−2.71	.01306	2.53	.04198
1970	1,087	.03122	1.41	−.17406	−12.63	.07731	4.94	.00634	1.26	.15209
1971	1,170	.12984	4.79	.03682	2.39	−.02034	−1.42	−.00531	.72	.00476
1972	1,247	.06297	3.38	.00048	.06	−.03897	−2.61	.01351	2.15	.00734
1973	1,333	−.12822	−6.70	−.12818	−14.85	−.01026	−1.16	.00419	1.00	.14858
1974	1,369	−.37344	−23.03	.03013	5.71	.00758	1.21	−.00044	−.07	.02221
1975	1,395	.27547	8.73	.21997	11.35	−.00442	−.87	−.02988	−2.14	.08849
1976	1,414	.26785	13.53	.05822	6.85	.01772	3.45	−.02079	−2.83	.05333
1977	1,448	.07667	5.64	−.00432	−.41	.01261	2.30	−.02001	−4.20	.01470
1978	1,480	−.10388	−5.06	.12157	10.06	.02822	4.77	−.00183	−.30	.08338
1979	1,509	.11108	3.54	.13578	7.05	.01002	1.06	−.01442	−1.71	.03615
1980	1,538	.03765	1.31	.17102	8.89	−.02761	−3.27	.00433	.57	.05678
1981	1,597	−.14340	−9.07	.03684	4.35	.00644	1.29	−.01028	−2.30	.01546
$\bar{\gamma}_j$		.04623		.05277		.01784		−.00929		.05638
$t(\bar{\gamma}_j)$		.94		2.13		1.71		02.01		
$p[|t(\bar{\gamma}_j)|]$		3.58		.046		.103		.059		

Note: R_j denotes the annual realized rate of return on stock j; R_f, the riskless rate of interest; β_j, the estimated systematic risk coefficient of stock j; D_j, firm j's long-term debt to total market value of equity ratio; and S_j, the total market value of firm j's common stock.

Table 6A-26
Summary of Cross-Sectional Regression Results of the Ex Post Sharpe-Lintner Model with Price per Share Included as an Additional Explanatory Variable

$$R_j - R_f = .\hat{\gamma}_0 + \hat{\gamma}_1\beta_j + \hat{\gamma}_2 P_j$$

Year	Number of Observations	$\hat{\gamma}_0$	$t(\hat{\gamma}_0)$	$\hat{\gamma}_1$	$t(\hat{\gamma}_1)$	$\hat{\gamma}_2$	$t(\hat{\gamma}_2)$	$\bar{R}^2$
1963	677	.09401	5.77	.05133	5.05	.00022	.88	.03570
1964	718	.13892	7.92	.02621	2.58	-.00026	-1.06	.00796
1965	766	.11814	2.78	.23677	11.71	-.00338	-4.29	.18529
1966	815	-.22955	-9.94	.10918	7.64	-.00001	-.03	.06476
1967	852	.92063	12.61	.08906	2.49	-.01195	-8.51	.09361
1968	919	.54205	12.90	.02457	1.01	-.00738	-10.25	.10105
1969	981	-.27516	-10.09	-.05970	-4.46	.00238	5.46	.05743
1970	1,087	.06477	2.82	-.17939	-12.97	-.00048	-1.17	.13425
1971	1,170	.12121	3.68	.03646	2.30	-.00020	.31	.00362
1972	1,247	-.00167	.08	.00276	.33	.00188	3.64	.00898
1973	1,333	-.17980	-8.63	-.12230	-14.26	.00151	4.13	.15837
1974	1,369	-.34759	-20.63	.02940	5.59	-.00094	-1.72	.02398
1975	1,395	.36562	10.08	.19612	10.06	-.00665	-5.33	.10412
1976	1,414	.37535	15.46	.04841	5.59	-.00512	-6.69	.06940
1977	1,448	.15739	10.78	.00389	.38	-.00477	-9.19	.05412
1978	1,480	-.03671	-1.46	.11972	9.75	-.00223	-3.09	.07569
1979	1,509	.21070	5.38	.12680	6.57	-.00521	-4.02	.04435
1980	1,538	-.03353	-1.00	.17906	9.32	-.00208	-2.07	.05307
1981	1,597	-.04365	-2.23	.03538	4.26	-.00477	-7.67	.04679
$\bar{\gamma}_i$		.10322		.05020		-.00233		.06961
$t(\bar{\gamma}_i)$		1.50		2.13		-2.62		
$p[t(\bar{\gamma}_i)]$		.151		.046		.017		

Note: R_j denotes the annual realized rate of return on stock j; R_f, the riskless rate of interest; β_j, the estimated systematic risk of stock j; and P_j, the price per share of stock j.

Table 6A–27
Summary of Simple Correlation Coefficient Estimates between Firm Size and Price per Share

Year	Number of Observations ·	Correlation Coefficient, $\hat{r}$	$t(\hat{r})$
1963	677	.22134	5.90
1964	718	.19800	5.41
1965	766	.41043	12.44
1966	815	.42903	13.54
1967	852	.47386	15.69
1968	919	.46018	15.70
1969	981	.45709	16.08
1970	1,087	.54232	21.26
1971	1,170	.53398	21.58
1972	1,247	.54786	23.11
1973	1,333	.55043	24.05
1974	1,369	.54556	24.07
1975	1,395	.53300	23.51
1976	1,414	.54348	24.33
1977	1,448	.52839	23.67
1978	1,480	.51762	23.26
1979	1,509	.39858	16.87
1980	1,538	.38261	16.23
1981	1,597	.39736	17.29
Mean		.45637	

Table 6A–28
Summary of Cross-Sectional Regression Results of the Ex Post Sharpe-Lintner Model with Price per Share and Firm Size Included as Additional Explanatory Variables

$$R_j = R_f + \hat{Y}_0 + \hat{\gamma}_1 \beta_j + \hat{\gamma}_2 P_j + \hat{\gamma}_3 S_j$$

Year	Number of Observations	$\hat{\gamma}_0$	$t(\hat{\gamma}_0)$	$\hat{\gamma}_1$	$t(\hat{\gamma}_1)$	$\hat{\gamma}_2$	$t(\hat{\gamma}_2)$	$\hat{\gamma}_3$	$t(\hat{\gamma}_3)$	$\bar{R}^2$
1963	677	.09310	5.69	.05125	5.04	.00017	.69	.00629	.77	.03511
1964	718	.13943	7.92	.02624	2.58	−.00024	−.97	−.00273	−.39	.00678
1965	766	.11815	2.76	.23677	11.70	−.00338	−3.92	.00002	.00	.18422
1966	815	−.23015	−9.91	.10903	7.61	.00003	.08	−.00146	−.25	.06368
1967	852	.92743	12.57	.08881	2.48	.01244	−7.83	.01618	.66	.09301
1968	919	.54678	13.00	.02989	1.22	.00799	−9.81	.01851	1.60	.10259
1969	981	−.27400	−9.96	−.05944	−4.43	.00231	4.75	.00187	.33	.05656
1970	1,087	.06553	2.83	−.17889	−12.85	.00039	.81	.00193	.32	.13353
1971	1,170	.11770	3.51	.03665	2.31	.00003	.04	−.00493	−.57	.00304
1972	1,247	.00024	.01	.00279	.33	.00175	2.84	.00301	.40	.00832
1973	1,333	−.18216	−8.72	−.12333	−14.33	.00181	4.18	−.00643	−1.30	.15881
1974	1,369	−.34536	−20.27	.02965	5.63	.00126	−1.94	.00707	.90	.02384
1975	1,395	.37082	10.09	.19510	9.99	.00733	−4.98	.01418	.87	.10396
1976	1,414	.37814	15.30	.04819	5.56	.00542	−5.98	.00525	.61	.06899
1977	1,448	.15885	10.66	.00407	.39	.00492	−8.06	.00268	.49	.05362
1978	1,480	−.03161	−1.24	.11983	9.76	.00276	−3.30	.00878	1.25	.07604
1979	1,509	.20985	5.34	.12656	6.54	.00508	−3.62	−.00219	−.24	.04375
1980	1,538	−.03353	−.99	.17906	9.30	.00208	1.91	.00002	.00	.05245
1981	1,597	−.04259	−2.17	.03589	4.31	.00495	−7.32	.00323	.68	.04646
$\bar{\gamma}_i$		.10456		.05043		−.00248		.00375		.06920
$t(\bar{\gamma}_i)$		1.51		2.15		−2.67		2.38		
$p[t(\bar{\gamma}_i)]$		.148		.045		.015		.028		

Note: R_j denotes the annual realized rate of return of stock j; R_f, the riskless rate of interest; β_j, the estimated systematic risk coefficient of stock j; P_j, the price per share of stock j; and S_j, the total market value of firm j's common stock.

7
Summary and Conclusions

I n this book we have sought to provide an analytical framework and empirical evidence on a variety of issues dealing with small business financing and taxation. Our principal objectives may be summarized in three questions:

1. What are the factors, other than taxes, that determine the methods by which the business activities of small, as compared with large, firms are financed?
2. What is the nature and magnitude of effective taxation of small, as compared with large, firms, and how does tax policy affect the financial policy of small, as compared with large, firms?
3. What have been the stock market returns to investors in small publicly traded firms as compared with the returns of investors in large publicly traded firms?

With respect to the first question, we conclude, in chapter 1, that a variety of factors, other than taxes, can affect the financial policy of small firms. The observed reluctance of small firms to seek outside equity financing and the reliance of small firms on debt financing, particularly bank loan financing, is explained by the relatively higher explicit and implicit costs of public equity financing. The explicit costs include the flotation and transaction costs faced in the primary and secondary markets. The implicit costs include the costs of monitoring the manager of the firm and of dealing with the information asymmetries that exist between the manager and the supplier of funds. Small firms seek out public financing only when the growth of the firm demands a broadening of the financial base beyond the limits imposed by bank lending.

The second question is addressed in chapters 2 through 5. On the basis of a model incorporating the effect of corporate and personal taxation, we conclude that corporations with low statutory tax rates, or with low probabilities of paying taxes (as a result of a lack of income), tend to issue less debt than corporations with high tax rates and/or with high probabilities of paying taxes. A similar conclusion is reached in the model of the relationship between firm size and capital structure that is developed in chapter 3. If a large firm is viewed as a portfolio of small firms (subsidiaries), the cash flows of which are less than perfectly positively correlated, then for a given level of assurance of full tax shield usage, a large firm will be able to choose a higher level of debt than a small firm because its cash flow is relatively less variable.

Empirical evidence on the differential effects of federal taxation is examined in chapter 4. For the years 1973–1979, data from *Statistics of Income—Corporation Income Tax Returns* classified by 11 asset size categories and 8 industrial divisions are examined. For the year 1976, data from the IRS *Source Book*, which provides more detailed information, were also examined. The principal conclusion is that small firms benefit less from tax deductions like interest expense than large firms. Small firms also benefit less from changes in the tax code that accelerate depreciation or that otherwise allow increased deductions from income. These conclusions are based on several pieces of evidence:

1. Small firms have lower statutory tax rates than large firms and, hence, have lower marginal tax benefits from deductions.
2. Small firms have greater variability of income than large firms and, hence, have a greater probability of not having sufficient income against which to take deductions.
3. Small firms tend to take proportionately less of the tentative investment tax credit than large firms and, hence, are less likely to have sufficient income to use the available tax credit.
4. Small firms appear to have a larger fraction of cash flow taken as depreciation and, hence, are likely to benefit less from further acceleration in depreciation.

These results imply that the Economic Recovery Tax Act (ERTA) of 1981, which reduces taxes by raising the level of allowable deductions like depreciation, benefits small firms less than large firms. While safe-harbor leasing provisions of ERTA allowed unused tax deductions to be sold, the Tax Equity and Fiscal Responsibility Act (TEFRA) of 1982 severely limited this practice and thereby made it more difficult for firms without income to realize tax benefits. However, recent proposals by the Treasury Department to eliminate accelerated depreciation and the investment tax credit would harm small firms less than large firms since small firms have greater difficulty in utilizing available tax deductions.

While the differential impact on small and large firms of federal taxation is quite clear and consistent with our expectations, empirical evidence on the significance of this differential impact for financial policy of small and large firms is less clear and is contrary to our expectations. In particular, regression analyses, carried in chapter 4 using 1976 data for four-digit industries and 10 asset size categories, indicate that the use of debt financing is negatively associated with the effective tax rate, positively associated with the level of depreciation expense, and positively associated with the firm size. While there are plausible explanations for these results, they are contrary to our expectations based on the effective taxes. Additional empirical work for other years is desirable to determine if these puzzling results hold up.

In addition to capital structure policy, an important financial policy of a corporation is the method by which earnings are paid out. Chapter 4 concludes with evidence on corporate payout policy. The tax return data indicate that the largest firms tend to have the highest dividend payout as compared with firms of other sizes. Service firms are an exception to this trend. Small firms usually pay out profits in the form of excess salary rather than dividends, something which may compensate for the lower dividend payment of small firms. We were unable to discover any consistency across major industrial divisions in the relationship of dividend payout to other financial variables of the firm such as short run profitability and cash availability. However, this should not be too surprising since many unobservable factors are likely to affect dividend policy. Particularly for small firms, the dividend payout will depend on circumstances of the owner of the firm for which no data are available. In addition, the tax return data have drawbacks because firms are aggregated into industries and size categories and because a snapshot of one year at a time is provided. Dividend payout is likely to be based on permanent cash flow, something that is difficult to estimate without time series data for individual firms.

Time series data for publicly traded firms are available on COMPUSTAT. With this data set a more sophisticated analysis of the determinants of corporate capital structure was possible than with the tax return data. The empirical results in chapter 5 are, nevertheless, mixed and are sensitive to the variable used to measure capital structure and to the inclusion of a dividend payout variable. While the regression results are not consistent from year to year, the regression with the greatest explanatory power on average indicates that leverage decreases with income variability and increases with firm size (as predicted by the model). Leverage also appears to be positively related to depreciation expense (contrary to the model's prediction) and to dividend payout.

Answers to the third question are provided in chapter 6. Recent empirical evidence indicates that the risk-adjusted rate of return to investors in the stocks of small firms exceeds that of investors in stocks of large firms. This size effect is inconsistent with the notion of an efficient capital market in which all securities of equal risk are expected to have equal rates of return. It also implies that the cost of equity capital is higher for small firms than for large firms. We confirm this size effect using stock market return data for NYSE, AMEX, and a few OTC firms for the period 1963 through 1981. Measures are then taken to reduce certain statistical biases that may exist in the test design. However, approximately one-half of the original size effect remains. The focus then turns to examining the effects of certain firm-specific financial policies as possible explainers of the cross-sectional differences in risk-adjusted return. Dividend yield, earnings yield, and the debt-equity ratio are considered. Differences in return are not related to dividend yield, are strongly positively related to earnings yield, and are marginally positively related to leverage. However, in all cases, the size variable also remains statistically significant, indicating that small firms have higher risk-adjusted returns. Only when stock price, a variable highly negatively correlated with secondary market transaction costs, is included in the regression does the effect of firm size change. This suggests that the higher secondary market transaction costs of small firms, rather than differences in financial policy, are responsible for the higher required stock market returns. Along with the evidence in chapter 1, this finding implies that the costs of public financing of small firms can be reduced by improving the operating efficiency of securities markets.

Bibliography

G. Akerlof, "The Market for 'Lemons': Qualitative Uncertainty and the Market Mechanism," *Quarterly Journal of Economics* 89 (August 1970):488–500.

S.S. Alexander, "The Effect of Size of Manufacturing Corporations on the Distribution of the Rate of Return," *Review of Economics and Statistics* 31 (1949):229–235.

A.J. Auerbach, "Stockholder Tax Rates, Size and Firm Financial Policy," Study conducted for Small Business Administration, Washington, D.C., December 1981, 41 pages.

R. Ball, "Anomalies in Relationships Between Securities' Yield and Yield Surrogates," *Journal of Financial Economics* 6 (1978):103–126.

R. Banz, "The Relationship Between Return and Market Value of Common Stocks," *Journal of Financial Economics* 9 (March 1981):3–18.

C.B. Barry and S.J. Brown, "Differential Information and the Small Firm Effect," Working Paper, Cox School of Business, Southern Methodist University, Dallas, Texas, 1982.

S. Basu, "Investment Performance of Common Stocks in Relation to Their Price-Earnings Ratios: A Test of the Efficient Market Hypothesis," *Journal of Finance* 32 (June 1977):663–682.

———, "The Relationship Between Earnings' Yield, Market Value and Return for NYSE Common Stocks: Further Evidence," *Journal of Financial Economics* 12 (June 1983):129–156.

A. Berges; J.J. McConnell; and G.G. Schlarbaum, "An Investigation of the Turn-of-the-Year Effect, the Small Firm Effect and the Tax-Loss-Selling Hypothesis in Canadian Stock Returns," Working Paper, Purdue University, West Lafayette, Indiana, 1982.

F. Black and M.S. Scholes, "The Effects of Dividend Yield and Dividend Policy on Common Stock Prices and Returns," *Journal of Financial Economics* 1 (March 1974):1–22.

M.E. Blume, "Stock Returns and Dividends Yields: Some More Evidence," *Review of Economics and Statistics* 62 (November 1980):567–577.

M.E. Blume and R.F. Stambaugh, "Biases in Computed Returns: An Application of the Size Effect," *Journal of Financial Economics* 12 (1983):387–404.

M.J. Brennan, "Investor Taxes, Market Equilibrium and Corporate Finance," Ph.D. diss., MIT, Cambridge, Mass., 1970a.

———, "Taxes, Market Valuation and Corporate Financial Policy," *National Tax Journal* 23 (December 1970b):417–427.

M.J. Brennan and E.S. Schwartz, "Corporate Income Taxes, Valuation, and the Problem of Optimal Capital Structure," *Journal of Business* 51 (January 1978):103–114.

P. Brown; D.B. Keim; A.W. Kleidon; and T.A. Marsh, "Stock Return Seasonalities and the Tax-Loss Selling Hypothesis: Analysis of the Arguments and Australian Evidence," *Journal of Financial Economics* 12 (June 1983):105–127.

P. Brown; A.W. Kleidon; and T.A. Marsh, "New Evidence on the Nature of Size-Related Anomalies in Stock Prices," *Journal of Financial Economics* 12 (June 1983):33–56.

T.S. Campbell, "Optimal Investment Financing Decisions and the Value of Confidentiality, *Journal of Financial and Quantitative Analysis* 14 (December 1979):913–924.

T.J. Cook and M.S. Rozeff, "Size, Dividend Yield and Co-Skewness Effects on Stock Returns: Some Empirical Tests," Working Paper 82-20, University of Iowa, Iowa City, 1982.

P. Cooley and C. Edwards, "Ownership Effects on Managerial Salaries in Small Business," *Financial Management* 11 (Winter 1982):5–9.

J.J. Cordes and S.M. Sheffrin, "Taxation and the Sectoral Allocation of Capital in the U.S.," *National Tax Journal* 34 (1981):419–432.

———, "Estimating the Tax Advantage of Corporate Debt," *Journal of Finance* 38 (March 1983):95–105.

A. Curley and H.R. Stoll, "The Small Business Equity Gap: An Empirical Study," Completed for the Small Business Administration, Washington, D.C., May 1968.

H. DeAngelo and R. Masulis, "Optimal Capital Structure Under Corporate and Personal Taxation," *Journal of Financial Economics* 8 (March 1980):3–29.

E. Dimson, "Risk Measurement When Shares Are Subject to Infrequent Trading," *Journal of Financial Economics* 7 (June 1979):197–226.

E.F. Fama, "Agency Problems and the Theory of the Firm," *Journal of Political Economy* 88 (April 1980):288–307.

E.F. Fama and M.C. Jensen, "Residual Claims and Investment Decisions," CRSP Working Paper, University of Chicago, September 1982a.

———, "Agency Problems and Residual Claims," Managerial Economics Research Center Working Paper, University of Rochester, Rochester, N.Y., December 1982b.

———, "Separation of Ownership and Control," *Journal of Law and Economics* 26 (June 1983):327–350.

M.S. Feldstein and J. Green, "Why Do Companies Pay Dividends," *American Economic Review* 73 (March 1983):17–30.

M.S. Feldstein and J. Slemrod, "Personal Taxation, Portfolio Choice and the Effect of the Corporation Income Tax," *Journal of Political Economy* 88 (October 1980):854–866.

L. Fisher, "Some New York Stock Market Indices," *Journal of Business* 39 (January 1966):191–225.

D.J. Fowler and C.H. Rorke, "Risk Measurement When Shares Are Subject to Infrequent Trading: Comment," *Journal of Financial Economics* 12 (August 1983):279–283.

K.R. French, "Stock Returns and the Weekend Effect," *Journal of Financial Economics* 8 (1980):55–69.

I. Friend and R. Westerfield, "Co-Skewness and Capital Asset Pricing," *Journal of Finance* 35 (September 1980):897–913.

I. Friend; R. Westerfield; and M. Granito, "New Evidence on the Capital Asset Pricing Model," *Journal of Finance* 33 (June 1978):903–920.

M.R. Gibbons and P. Hess, "Day of the Week Effects and Asset Returns," *Journal of Business* 54 (1981):579–596.

D. Givoly; R. Kumar; G.N. Mandelker; and S.G. Rhee, "The Small-Firm Effect: Some Evidence on the Price-Level Factor," Working Paper, University of Pittsburgh, July 1983.

R.H. Gordon and D.F. Bradford, "Taxation and the Stock Market Valuation of Capital Gains and Dividends," *Journal of Public Economics* 14 (April 1980):109–136.

R.S. Hamada, "Portfolio Analysis Market Equilibrium and Corporate Finance," *Journal of Finance* 24 (1969):13–31.

C. James and R.O. Edmister, "The Relationship Among Common Stocks, Trading Value and Market Value," *Journal of Finance* 38 (September 1983):1075–1086.

M.C. Jensen and W.H. Meckling, "Theory of the Firm: Managerial Behavior, Agency Costs and Ownership Structure," *Journal of Financial Economics* (October 1976):305–360.

D.B. Keim, "Dividend Yields and Stock Returns: Implications of Abnormal January Returns," Working Paper, The Wharton School, University of Pennsylvania, Philadelphia, 1983a.

———, "The Relation Between Day of the Week Effects and Size Effects," Working Paper, The Wharton School, University of Pennsylvania, Philadelphia, 1983b.

———, "Size-Related Anomalies and Stock Return Seasonality: Further Empirical Evidence," *Journal of Financial Economics* 12 (June 1983c):13–32.

H. Kim, "A Mean-Variance Theory of Optimal Capital Structure and Corporate Debt Capacity," *Journal of Finance* 33 (1978):45–64.

H. Kim; W. Lewellen; and J. McConnell, "Financial Leverage Clienteles: Theory and Evidence," *Journal of Financial Economics* 7 (1978):83–109.

A. Kraus and R.H. Litzenberger, "A State-Preference Model of Optimal Capital Structure," *Journal of Finance* 28 (September 1973):911–922.

———, "Skewness Preference and the Valuation of Risk Assets," *Journal of Finance* 31 (September 1976):253–268.

J. Lakonishok and M. Levi, "Weekend Effects on Stock Returns: A Note," *Journal of Finance* 37 (June 1982):883–889.

J. Lakonishok and A.C. Shapiro, "Partial Diversification as an Explanation of the Small Firm Effect," Working Paper, University of North Carolina, Chapel Hill, 1982.

J. Lakonishok and S. Smidt, "Volume and Turn of the Year Behavior," *Journal of Financial Economics* 13 (1984):435–455.

H.E. Leland and D.H. Pyle, "Informational Asymmetrics, Financial Structure, and Financial Intermediation," *Journal of Finance* 32 (May 1977):371–388.

J. Lintner, "The Valuation of Risk Assets and the Selection of Risky Investments in Stock Portfolios and Capital Budgets," *Review of Economics and Statistics* (February 1965):13–37.

R.H. Litzenberger and K. Ramaswamy, "The Effect of Personal Taxes and Dividends on Capital Asset Prices: Theory and Empirical Evidence," *Journal of Financial Economics* 7 (June 1979):163–95.

R.H. Litzenberger and J.C. Van Horne, "Elimination of the Double Taxation of Dividends and Corporate Financial Policy," *Journal of Finance* 33 (June 1978):737–750.

M.H. Miller, "Debt and Taxes," *Journal of Finance* 32 (May 1977):261–275.

M.H. Miller and F. Modigliani, "Dividend Policy, Growth and the Valuation of Shares," *Journal of Business* 34 (1961):411–433.

M.H. Miller and M.S. Scholes, "Rates of Return in Relation to Risk: A Re-Examination of Some Recent Empirical Findings," in *Studies in the Theory of Capital Markets*, M.C. Jensen, ed. (New York: Praeger, 1972):47–78.

———, "Dividends and Taxes," *Journal of Financial Economics* 6 (1978):333–364.

———, "Dividends and Taxes: Some Empirical Evidence," *Journal of Political Economy* 90 (December 1982a):1118–1141.

———, "Executive Compensation, Taxes, and Incentives," in *Financial Economics: Essays in Honor of Paul Cootner*, W.F. Sharpe and P. Cootner, eds. (Englewood Cliffs, N.J.: Prentice-Hall, 1982b).

F. Modigliani and M.H. Miller, "The Cost of Capital, Corporate Finance, and The Theory of Investment," *The American Economic Review* (June 1958):291–297.

———, "Corporate Income Taxes and the Cost of Capital: A Correction," *American Economic Review* (June 1963):433–443.

I.G. Morgan; A.L. MacBeth; and D.J. Novak, "The Relationship Between Equity Value and Abnormal Returns in the Canadian Stock Market," Working Paper 81-12, Queen's University, Kingston, Ontario, Canada 1982.

S. Myers, "Determinants of Corporate Borrowing," *Journal of Financial Economics* 4 (1977):147–176.

G. Ragazzi, "On the Relation Between Ownership Dispersion and the Firm's Market Value," *Journal of Banking and Finance* 5 (1981):261–276.

M.R. Reinganum, "Misspecification of Capital Asset Pricing: Empirical Anomalies Based on Earnings' Yields and Market Values," *Journal of Financial Economics* 9 (March 1981a):19–46.

———,"Abnormal Returns in Small Firm Portfolios," *Financial Analysts Journal* (March-April 1981b):52–56.

———, "A Direct Test of Roll's Conjecture on the Firm Size Effect," *Journal of Finance* (March 1982):27–35.

———, "The Anomalous Stock Market Behavior of Small Firms in January: Empirical Tests for Tax-Loss Selling Effects," *Journal of Financial Economics* 12 (June 1983):89–104.

A. Robichek and S. Myers, "Problems in the Theory of Optimal Capital Structure," *Journal of Financial and Quantitative Analysis* 1 (1966):1–35.

R.J. Rogalski, "New Findings Regarding Day of the Week Returns Over Trading and Non-Trading Periods: A Note," *Journal of Finance* 39 (December 1984):1603–1614.

R. Roll, "A Possible Explanation of the Small Firm Effect," *Journal of Finance* 36 (September 1981):879–888.

———, "On Computing Mean Returns and the Small Firm Premium," *Journal of Financial Economics* 12 (1983a):371–386.

———, "Vas Ist Das? The Turn of the Year Effect and the Return Premium of Small Firms," *Journal of Portfolio Management* 9 (1983b):18–28.

———, "A Simple Implicit Measure of the Effective Bid/Ask Spread in an Efficient Market," *Journal of Finance* 39 (September 1984):1127–1139.

S.A. Ross, "The Determination of Financial Structure: The Incentive-Signalling Approach," *Bell Journal of Economics* (Spring 1977):23–40.

———, "Some Notes on Financial Structure: The Incentive-Signalling Models, Activity Choice and Risk Preferences," *Journal of Finance* 33 (June 1978):777–792.

M.E. Rubinstein, "A Mean-Variance Synthesis of Corporate Financial Theory," *Journal of Finance* 28 (March 1973):167–181.

M. Schneller, "Taxes and the Optimal Capital Structure of the Firm," *Journal of Finance* 35 (1980):119–127.

G.W. Schwert, "Size and Stock Returns, and Other Empirical Regularities," *Journal of Financial Economics* 12 (June 1983):3–12.

J. Scott, "A Theory of Optimal Capital Structure," *Bell Journal of Economics and Management Science* 7 (1976):33–54.

Securities and Exchange Commission, *Initial Public Offerings of Common Stock: The Role of Regional Brokers–Dealers in the Capital Formation Process*, Phase I Report (March 1980), Washington, D.C.

M.S. Scholes and J. Williams, "Estimating Betas From Nonsynchronous Data," *Journal of Financial Economics* 5 (December 1977):309–327.

W.F. Sharpe, "Capital Asset Prices: A Theory of Market Equilibrium Under Conditions of Risk," *Journal of Finance* 19 (September 1964):425–442.

H.O. Stekler, *Profitability and Size of Firm*, Institute of Business and Economic Research, University of California, Berkeley, August 1963.

E.J. Stockwell and Byrnes, "Small Business Financing Corporate Manufacturers," *Federal Reserve Bulletin* (January 1961):44–48.

H.R. Stoll, "The Supply of Dealer Services in Securities Markets," *The Journal of Finance* 33 (September 1978a):1133–1151.

———, "The Pricing of Security Dealer Services: An Empirical Study of NASDAQ Stocks," *Journal of Finance* 33 (September 1978b):1153–1172.

———, "Commodity Futures and Spot Price Determination and Hedging in Capital Market Equilibrium," *Journal of Financial and Quantitative Analysis* 14 (November 1979):873–894.

———, "Small Firms' Access to Public Equity Financing," Background study prepared for Interagency Task Force on Small Business Finance, February 1982, Washington, D.C.

H.R. Stoll and A. Curley, "Small Business and the New Issues Market of Equities," *Journal of Financial Quantitative Analysis* 5 (September 1970):309–322.

H.R. Stoll and J. Walter, "Tax Incentives for Small Business," Heller Small Business Institute Policy Paper No. 1, November 1980, Chicago, Illinois.

H.R. Stoll and R.E. Whaley, "Transaction Costs and the Small Firm Effect," *Journal of Financial Economics* (June 1983):57–79.

A.O. Trostel and M.L. Nichols, "Privately-Held and Publicly-Held Companies: A Comparison of Strategic Choices and Management Processes," *Academy of Management Journal* 25 (March 1982):47–62.

U.S. Internal Revenue Service (IRS), *Source Book, Statistics of Income, Corporation Income Tax Returns*, 1976, Washington, D.C.

U.S. Internal Revenue Service (IRS), *Statistics of Income, Corporation Income Tax Returns*, various editions, 1973–1979, Washington, D.C.

J. Warner, "Bankruptcy Costs: Some Evidence," *Journal of Finance* 32 (May 1977):337–347.

Index

About the Authors

Theodore E. Day is assistant professor of management at Vanderbilt University's Owen Graduate School of Management, where he teaches courses in investment management and corporate finance. A certified public accountant, Professor Day holds an M.B.A. from the University of Oklahoma and a Ph.D. in finance from Stanford University's Graduate School of Business. Professor Day has published research examining the effect of inflation on interest rates and stock prices. He has been a member of the faculty of Vanderbilt University since 1981.

Hans R. Stoll is the Anne Marie and Thomas B. Walker, Jr., Professor of Finance at the Owen Graduate School of Management, Vanderbilt University. Prior to coming to Vanderbilt in 1980, he was at the Wharton School of the University of Pennsylvania where he had been a member of the faculty since 1966. He received an A.B. degree from Swarthmore College in 1961 and M.B.A. and Ph.D. degrees from the Graduate School of Business of the University of Chicago in 1963 and 1966, respectively. He has also been a Senior Fulbright–Hays Act Visiting Lecturer in France and has served on the staff of the Institutional Investor Study of the Securities and Exchange Commission. Professor Stoll has published articles on subjects including options, commodity futures, small business financing, the impact of institutional investors on the stock market, the theory of dealers in securities markets, foreign exchange rates, and stock market returns of small firms.

Robert E. Whaley is associate professor of finance and director of the Institute for Financial Research at the University of Alberta. From 1978 to 1984, he was on the faculty of the Owen Graduate School of Management, Vanderbilt University. Professor Whaley received a B.Com. degree from the University of Alberta in 1975 and M.B.A. and Ph.D. degrees from the University of Toronto in 1976 and 1978, respectively. Professor Whaley has published articles on the valuation of options, the anticipation of quarterly earnings announcements, the stock market returns of small firms, and options on futures.